The Dot-Com Decision

The Dot-Com Decision

*How to Evaluate the Company,
the Compensation, and the Culture
in Today's High-Stakes Job Market*

Robert F. Wilson

McGraw-Hill

New York   Chicago   San Francisco
Lisbon   London   Madrid   Mexico City
Milan   New Delhi   San Juan   Seoul
Singapore   Sydney   Toronto

McGraw-Hill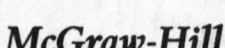
A Division of The McGraw·Hill Companies

Copyright © 2002 by Robert F. Wilson. All rights reserved. Printed in the United States of America. Except as permitted under the United States Copyright Act of 1976, no part of this publication may be reproduced or distributed in any form or by any means, or stored in a data base or retrieval system, without the prior written permission of the publisher.

1 2 3 4 5 6 7 8 9 0   DOC/DOC   0 9 8 7 6 5 4 3 2 1

ISBN 0-07-137587-2

The material on pages 119–140 was written by WetFeet.com, Inc., a provider of independent research and information about companies, industries, and careers, and has been reprinted with permission. Copyright © 2001, WetFeet.com, Inc. For further information about this or other career-related topices, please visit www.wetfeet.com, call (800) 926-4562, or send an email to info@wetfeet.com.

This book was set in Granjon by Patricia Wallenburg.

Printed and bound by R.R. Donnelley & Sons.

McGraw-Hill books are available at special quantity discounts to use as premiums and sales promotions, or for use in corporate training programs. For more information, please write to the Director of Special Sales, Professional Publishing, McGraw-Hill, Two Penn Plaza, New York, NY 10121-2298. Or contact your local bookstore.

 This book is printed on recycled, acid-free paper containing a minimum of 50% recycled, de-inked fiber.

To Clifford and Mildred

Contents

Preface ix
Acknowledgments xiii

Part One
The Dot-Com Landscape:
A View from the Inside

1 The Internet: Where It's Going and How It Got Here 3
2 A Web in Full: Interconnected Companies, Overlapping Interests 23
3 E-Commerce Companies: Life on the Edge 33

Part Two
Dot-Com Diary:
Analysis of a Start-Up

4 Isolating a Market Niche: Framing a Mission 49

CONTENTS

5 The Power Brokers: Angels, Venture Capitalists, and Incubators 59
6 Building a Killer Management Team 73

Part Three
Identifying the Match: What It Takes to Fit In

7 Culture Shock Beyond Dress Code 83
8 What Kind of Job Are You Looking For? 97
9 Life in the Trenches: Six Professionals Tell Their Stories 119

Part Four
Getting the Job You Want

10 Marketing Brand You: What to Do with Your Targeted Résumé 143
11 Avoiding Interview Potholes 175
12 Negotiating Compensation 189
    Appendix: Stock Options and Restricted Stock 199
    Glossary 207
    Bibliography 215
    Index 219

Preface

If you're in a bookstore trying to decide whether to read *The Dot-Com Decision*, we'll try to help you telescope the process. First, if you view working for an Internet company as a practical career option, you'll need to be able to answer "yes" to one of the following questions:

Are you:

- A college student thinking about an Internet career, but uncertain as to how to best prepare for it?
- A recent college graduate whose studies point toward a yet-to-be-defined Internet career?
- A successful professional considering an Internet opportunity?
- A recently downsized or dissatisfied professional at a career crossroads?

Second, you need to know whether the information in this book answers the questions you have about careers in Internet companies. *The Dot-Com Decision*, for example, covers:

PREFACE

- The basics about working either in a dot-com start-up or in a more established Web company that's been around for a while. This book will tell you what to expect regarding corporate culture, compensation, and career path.
- The basic differences between a traditional brick-and-mortar company and an Internet company. This book will tell you how to distinguish between an established software company and a relatively new dot-com company, and between traditional media and new media.
- How to determine whether working in dot-com companies of various kinds is right for you. This book will tell you what temperament, skill sets, and risk-taking comfort level will offer the best prospects for a smooth transition.
- What strategies and methods are best to get on the Net career path of your choice. This book will tell you which job-search marketing strategies, interviewing styles, and résumé writing tips will be most relevant.

(Note to college students and recent graduates: *It may make sense for you to read Parts Three and Four of* The Dot-Com Decision—*where all the job preparation information is—before you read Parts One and Two. Read over the Table of Contents first to decide.)*

Between 1998 and 2008, occupations in Internet and other Web-related companies are projected by the U.S. Bureau of Labor Statistics to be the fastest growing among all industries. Of the 16 occupations in all industries projected to grow fastest during this 10-year period, in fact, eight of them are computer- or Internet-related.

Offsetting this optimistic projection is the wave of Internet company layoffs and dot-com start-up failures that began in the year 2000 and continued into 2001. Tens of thousands of workers have been affected, which makes due diligence (covered in Chapter 7: Culture Shock Beyond Dress Code) even more crucial in making a job-selection decision.

PREFACE

A number of Internet professionals share their experiences throughout *The Dot-Com Decision*. Among them are entrepreneurs, company founders, chief executive officers, and corporate vice presidents of various functions. We have also asked several officers from leading recruitment companies and Web sites to describe what they look for to successfully fill openings of various kinds. Their insights provide a human dimension to help you understand how good employees are identified and hired.

Please let us know what information in *The Dot-Com Decision* has been helpful to you in your search, as well as what you would have liked to see here but did not find. A movement so new, moving so fast, invites tectonic change. Some material written just weeks before it was printed here may be out of date by the time you read it. We'll catch up as best we can in the next edition, hoping that the pace of change may have decelerated just a bit.

Robert F. Wilson
bobwilson@job-bridge.com
www.job-bridge.com

Acknowledgments

A number of colleagues, friends, and Internet industry professionals have made significant contributions to the quality and vitality of this manuscript, among them: Martha Buchanan; Amy Brownstein, RLM; Dr. Timothy Collins, National Louis University; James DuBeau, Multicity.com; Susie Fong, WetFeet.com; Grace Freedson's Publishing Network; Lisa Glass, Hoover's Online; Mary Glenn, McGraw-Hill; Michelle Hellyar, Corporate Technology Communications; Richard Johnson, HotJobs.com; Rebecca Lawler, The Corporate Library; Mary Linley; Janice Race, McGraw-Hill; Erik Rambusch, Rambusch Associates; Audrey Reynolds, WetFeet.com; Kenneth Rivera; Christine Roberts, Richard A. Eisner & Company; Audrey Ronis-Tobin, Globix Corporation; Marcia Shin; Ashley Sizemore, Shoor & Company; Susan Sperry, Fleishman Hillard; Kavi Wright; Devra Zabot, HotJobs.com.

Occupation descriptions in Chapter 8 adapted from *Occupational Outlook Handbook* (2000–2001), courtesy U.S. Department of Labor, Bureau of Labor Statistics.

Material in Chapter 9 adapted courtesy of WetFeet.com, Inc., a provider of independent research and information about companies,

ACKNOWLEDGMENTS

industries, and careers; reprinted with permission. Copyright © 2001, WetFeet.com, Inc.

Material in Chapter 11 adapted from *Interview to Win, Second Edition*, and *Interview to Win Your First Job, Third Edition*, courtesy of Wilson McLeran, Inc. Copyright © 2000.

Sidebar selection and interview transcription courtesy of Martha Buchanan.

Appendix: "Stock Options and Restricted Stock," reprinted courtesy of Richard A. Eisner & Company, LLP.

PART ONE

The Dot-Com Landscape: A View from the Inside

The personal computer industry's growth from zero to $100 billion in 10 years is said to be the greatest legal accumulation of wealth in history. In another 5 years it is estimated that the Internet economy will reach $800 billion. Dot-com companies—those with 95 percent or more of their revenues derived from the Internet—make up less than 10 percent of the total Internet economy, though they seem to make most of the news. Where are the dot-coms going, and what part will they play in the total Internet economy?

CHAPTER ONE

The Internet: Where It's Going and How It Got Here

It took 40 years for radio to attract 50 million listeners. Television and cable TV viewers reached 50 million in 13 years. And in less than 6 years, 50 million people were surfing the Web. That's one powerful medium.

The Internet, experts say, will rival the Industrial Revolution for its impact on worldwide social and economic change. Already it is changing the way companies do business, and eventually it will change the way people live. Even so, only 1 percent of the world's population now has any kind of Internet capability, including e-mail. And just 10 percent of the world's personal computer (PC) users have Internet access, also including e-mail.

There are now millions of Web sites, and more than 1 billion Web pages. Early in 2001 the search engine Google had identified and catalogued 1,346,966,000 pages. The problem is that most of us access whatever number of these pages comprise our personal Web universe by using modems and telephone lines, which brings the entire process to a screeching halt—very un-Internetlike. But the new-media technologists promise us that bandwidth help is on the way. Internet2, they tell us (a partnership of universities, corporations, and government agencies formed in 1996), will change all that. Even now plans are being laid for high-speed networks that will transmit data 45,000 times faster than our modern-day Model T: the good old 56K modem.

Watching this volatile and paradoxical phenomenon unfold even before dawn has broken on the twenty-first century—at least the sliver of it any of us will witness in our lifetimes—is a little like watching the birth of real estate at Hawaii Volcanoes National Park. It is irrevocable, beautiful, incomprehensible, and a little bit scary all at the same time.

A FLURRY OF FAILURE

So with such growing-pains-induced upheaval, it is no surprise that the dot-com landscape includes both thriving companies whose products or services have secured a viable niche—at least for the time being—and the smoking remains of others that have gone down hard for a variety of reasons. According to *The Industry Standard*, a computer industry trade publication, 210 start-up Internet companies ceased operations in the year 2000, with no letup in 2001. Other experts put the figure considerably higher.[1] Turnover became so furious that the magazine keeps running tallies of dead and dying companies—mostly dot-com start-ups—and the men and women who ran them. Daily links identify the losers through lists tagged Layoff Tracker, Flop Tracker, and Ex-Exec Tracker.

Reveling in the misery of dot-com failure begat a rash of Web sites dedicated to just that. Dotcomfailures.com, startupfailures.com, and Dotcom Graveyard (at Upside.com) are a few of them—destined mercifully to the same fate, as quickly as the Internet's first shakeout runs its course.

Only after several years of seemingly whimsical reasons for success or failure is a gold-rush mentality beginning to subside. *Seemingly* whimsi-

---

[1] An Applied Communications Research survey estimated that over 300 dot-coms announced closures in 2000.

> ## What's in a Name?
>
> The dot-com crash has created a garage sale for customer lists, technology, and distribution centers. But now we have hard evidence that the debacle has reached its nadir. Dot-coms are selling what's equivalent to the siding off the house: their URLs.
>
> In a last-ditch effort to squeeze more money out of this market, several publicly traded dot-coms shutting their doors are putting their domain names on the block. But what are those names actually worth? Alas, not much. "There is a surfeit of names, but nobody wants to buy them," says Peter Sealey, an adjunct professor at the Haas Marketing Group at the University of California at Berkeley. "Companies are throwing assets out there and getting no takers."
>
> —Lisa Meyer
> RedHerring.com

cal because many professional reputations have suffered, along with savings accounts and solvency. ("LOST $6B IN A DAY" whooped a front page banner in the New York *Daily News* one March 2000 morning, above a photo of the chagrined executive. "Hotshot tech CEO loses fortune as his company's stock plunges 140 points.") Similar stories by the hundreds, just as smugly told, have been fully as painful to those involved, but most not nearly as public.

Paul Rand, founder and CEO of Chicago-based Corporate Technology Communications, believes that inexperience is a major factor in such failures, and that the majority of entrepreneurs who run successful businesses make it on their third or fourth attempts, rather than the first or second.

"The hope is to make your bigger idiotic mistakes early on—and learn from them," says Rand. "The number one reason most start-ups fail is that they're based on unsound business models. Number two is the inexperience of the founders and the leaders. Those two factors combined, plus the obvious lack of market need, end up being a pretty lethal combination."

Still, the dot-com horror story does have another perspective. During the same period early in 2001 that eliminated hundreds of dot-com jobs, brick-and-mortar grounded companies such as DaimlerChrysler, General Electric, and Motorola (and dozens of others) let go tens of thousands of people. Even so, this was difficult to detect based on national press coverage. A single-month journalistic biopsy conducted by *Business2.0* counters the gleeful spin afforded the "dot-bomb" saga as exemplified by three leading national daily newspapers. Editor Tessa Romita and a team of reporters determined that the ratio of non-dot-com layoffs to dot-com layoffs was 30:1 from January 1 to February 1. Naturally it would be expected that the number of stories about these layoffs during this same period also would be close to 30:1. Instead, after a painstaking count, Romita's team found that the ratio was roughly 2:1 for the *New York Times*, 3:2 for the *Wall Street Journal*, and 1:1 for the *Washington Post*.

BUT WHAT IF THE GLASS IS HALF FULL?

Disciples of Net gloom seemingly lurk in every corner, but Peter J. Clark, author of *Net Value: Valuing Dot-Com Companies* and a partner at VBM Consulting (www.vbm-consulting.com), is not one of them. "I'm very positive about the Internet. Every major revolutionary economic development has crashed and burned after 6 or 7 years—and then rebounded."

Clark sees the rebound starting with online infrastructure leaders Cisco and Juniper. "They're still trying to overcome some disastrous acquisition decisions from the late nineties," he says, "but you've got to look beyond the present aberration."

"Everywhere I've interviewed lately," says Clark, "whether it's CNN or TheStreet.com, there seems to be interest in dot-coms only if we talk about how dead they are. Well, there happens to be another story. I say either buy online infrastructure for the next phase of the Net, or disappear and miss the *real* Net boom that's just over the horizon."

In a story for eCompany (www.ecompany.com) titled "Second Coming" in June 2001, Erick Schonfeld makes his own strong case for Net survival. Here are three brief excerpts:

> *Web technology could become intriguing once again—and if you listen carefully, you might even hear the faint chortling of engineers unable to contain their enthusiasm.... That's because the industry may be on the cusp of taking another technological leap forward—a step that, incidentally, wouldn't have been possible had it not been for all that hype and frittered-away cash that we all moan about today....*
>
> *New standards such as XML (extensible markup language), UDDI (universal description, discovery, and integration), and SOAP (simple object access protocol) are paving the way for an era when computers can call up data from Web servers and other connected computers on the fly with no human intervention. Variations of XML will even allow one computer to ask another to perform certain software tasks on its behalf. So a travel Web site could hook directly into, say, Sabre's airline reservation system and show the results as though the Sabre program were part of its own homegrown system, without going through the hassle of having a Web programmer hand-stitch the two applications together.*
>
> *Microsoft, perhaps more than any other company, is staking its future on these kinds of software services becoming a reality. Placing these developments under the rubric ".Net" [see Chapter 4], Microsoft sees the opportunity for creation of endless new Web services based on this ability to automatically share data and software processing between computers—especially those computers sitting at the edge of the Internet—your PC, primarily.*

TWO MODELS FOR ENDURING

Amid the carnage of dot-com failure in 2000 and 2001, it is easy to forget that large numbers of start-ups rewarded the faith—and funding—of their backers and are flourishing today. San Francisco–based market analyst Vernon Keenan (www.keenanvision.com) projected that the 8 million–plus U.S. businesses with fewer than 100 employees would account for more than $6 trillion in sales for 2001 compared to $5.5 trillion for all of the 10,000-plus-employee companies. There is no lack of recipes for success, to be sure. Here are two.

Multicity.com

In 1999, brothers Alain and Patrick Hanash, after months of research and experimentation in a makeshift basement office in their parents' home, devised an idea for an enterprise that within 2 years attracted $16 million in funding. The vision they shared, which they named Multicity (www.multicity.com), was based in two globalizing realizations:

- More than 52 percent of the earth's Internet users are non-English-speaking.
- By the year 2003, $913 billion in e-commerce revenue will be derived outside the United States—two-thirds of all global revenues.

The Hanash brothers married this worldview to an application service provider (ASP) model using technology that allows them to sell software and tools directly to Web sites, bypassing portals altogether. In essence, each participating Web site *becomes* a portal. This means that Multicity's users are able to contact users on any other sites that similarly use its tools and thus create the first multilingual open global network for communications tools.

Today Multicity's products include instant translation-enabled chat rooms (available in 17 languages), message boards, instant messaging (also with instant translation), auctions, and Web polls. Because some 80 percent of U.S. companies currently transact business online in

English only, Alain and Patrick Hanash have good reason to believe they're on to something. Further confirmation of their optimism was an award to Multicity from *Yahoo! Internet Life* magazine for "Best Chat" of 2001.

Insala Group

What Keenan Vision and other close observers of the Web say is that the more modest dot-com start-ups will offer interesting employment alternatives, but only for those able to accomplish a lot with few resources. These opportunistic entrepeneurs already have a label, as you may suspect: They've been dubbed "microdots." Whether that name sticks or not, these small companies able to use the Web well are either already showing profit or are on a path leading to black.

In 1999, a 4-year-old human resources consulting company joined forces with a Web developer in business for 2 years, forming Insala Group (www.insala.com). With just two employees each, the merged companies easily met the definition of a microdot.

Insala works in two business industries. In its human resources focus, the company fulfills executive search and staffing assignments. It also offers an interactive outplacement management instrument to ease the transition of those who have lost jobs in the wake of the downsizing patterns that seem now to be a permanent part of the corporate fabric. Clients include not only outplacement firms themselves but also universities, government agencies, and individuals. Insala also designs and hosts Web sites for corporate and university clients.

Says Phillip Roark, Insala CEO, "Out goal was to deliver high-quality, cost-effective Internet technologies in the two arenas in which we started—and we've done that. Currently we're growing at the rate of 16 percent per month, have 13 employees, and have just opened an office in Germany. But I'm also proud that we were able to fund this on our own, without outside assistance."

Inside View

Gary Alpert, Cofounder and CEO, WetFeet.com

With partner and president Steve Pollock, Gary Alpert founded the San Francisco–based career portal WetFeet.com (http://www.wetfeet.com) in 1994. Why Wet Feet? The inspiration came from Maine mail order magnate L.L. Bean, who started his own company two generations earlier by designing and manufacturing the first dry boot, thus liberating outdoorsmen and outdoorswomen the world over from wet feet forever. WetFeet.com (the metaphor) is committed to providing a dry-boot equivalence for both job seekers and corporate employers.

Q Based on the contact you maintain with human resources people around the country, how would you characterize the recent dot-com shakeout?

A I can give you a macro-level answer: It's certainly not over. I think there were a couple of years when anything with a "dot-com-ness" to it appeared to have nowhere to go but up. The money was there, and the perception—particularly among younger job candidates—was that the reward-to-risk ratio was good enough to make this a logical career choice. There is an awareness now, though, that companies growing that fast must rely on the capital markets to grow—and if the capital isn't there, they will contract instead. Our recent research with student job seekers shows almost a 180-degree shift in their industries of choice. They're back to looking at things like consulting, banking, and a lot of the more traditional firms because the perception is that they'll be safer there.

Q How much does this have to do with the drastic high-tech downsizings that began early in 2001?

A I think the media has focused its attention more on the Internet and dot-com arena, but these layoffs are occurring across the board. Dot-coms are most significantly impacted because they're smaller and have to scramble for capital even in the best of times. And obviously if you don't think the stock options are going to be worth anything, the jobs

continued on next page

are less attractive. This is going to be painful for a while, but once things settle down, the companies that remain will be in a much better position to thrive.

Q What distinctive hiring practices might a recruitment and career management company like WetFeet have?
A We've been pretty focused over the years in building a company that is certainly an Internet company, yet we have a very real business that existed long before the Internet became a real force in recruiting. We have corporate customers, we have consumer customers, we have revenues—we have the things that always used to matter in business, and that still matter today. So I think the folks who have joined us are drawn to the mission of the company, which is that we produce products that help people and help companies, and the fact that we have a robust business model. They like that about our company and also being part of an entrepreneurial opportunity. These are the kinds of people we have attracted. We're still at the size where everyone knows everyone else, and everyone knows that their work really matters.

Q How do you make sure you attract the best people?
A Probably our most significant recruitment mechanism is the referral program we've had in place since we started. The research is pretty consistent that the most effective recruitment engine is to hire the best people and for *them* to recruit good people they know. We reward team members when they refer people we hire who stay for at least 3 months. We also use the technology of our WetFeet recruitment system. There are customers who use our site and then decide they'd like to come work for us. So we make it easy for them to throw their hats in the ring. Everybody we interview talks to several people on the team. They need to know what it's like to work here not just from a human resources perspective. Our whole business is about educating job seekers to find out not only what is good about a job they're interested in but also what some of the challenges are that they might not like—and then making a decision after weighing all the factors.

continued on next page

> Q What does your crystal ball say about where WetFeet is going over the next few years?
>
> A We will work with more companies and more candidates, and we will expand our services to both. The only thing predictable about an economy is that sometimes things go up and sometimes they go down. Our site actually has remained popular under both scenarios. In fact, the site is stronger today than it ever has been. There are many job boards to visit, but job seekers are saying, "Well, I can get plenty of listings on job boards, but that's not going to tell me what I need to know about being happy in a job." Similarly, companies come to WetFeet because we can connect them to the high-caliber talent that is very difficult to reach on the mass boards.
>
> Depending on which statistic you believe, between 2 and 4 years is the average tenure in a job these days. Any way you look at it, this is a significant investment in a person's professional life. So it makes sense to spend time getting a real understanding of the industry, the companies, and the role you would play in them. In other words, to go into your discussions as an educated consumer. That's how people who know us view WetFeet: We're a *Consumer Reports* for job seekers and an end-to-end recruiting solutions provider for corporations.

HOW IT ALL BEGAN

So where did it come from: this worldwide broadcasting system, this mechanism for information dissemination, this medium for collaboration and interaction between individuals and their computers without regard for geography? Some credit Vannevar Bush, director of the Office of Scientific Search and Development, as being the first to foresee the World Wide Web. His ideas in an *Atlantic Monthly* article in July 1945, called "As We May Think," described the inevitability of a system of interconnected information access.

Other historians trace the Internet's roots to 1957. That was the year the Soviet Union launched Sputnik, the earth's first artificial satellite.

THE INTERNET: WHERE IT'S GOING AND HOW IT GOT HERE

> ### Roads That Were Built by Ike
>
> "I like Ike" was an irresistible slogan in 1952. About half a century later, there are reasons to "like Ike" even more....
>
> In 1957, while responding to the threat of the Soviets in general and the success of Sputnik in particular, President Dwight Eisenhower created both the Interstate Highway System and the Advanced Research Projects Agency, or ARPA.
>
> —*Steve Driscoll*
> *Online Computer Library Center*

Alarmed at potential consequences, the U.S. Department of Defense responded by creating the Advanced Research Projects Agency, which led in turn to the creation of a computer network designed to function even after a nuclear war, which was thought to be the worst-case scenario resulting from Sputnik and its progeny.

The contributors to *A Nation Transformed by Information* set this phenomenon in a much broader context.[2] They maintain that ground was laid for Bill Gates, e-mail, and digital architecture back in colonial times, when several primal information highways were created. The original architects were the Puritans, whose drive for universal literacy would—it was thought—make Bible study accessible to all.

Some time after this, several combinations of government action, breakthrough technology, and organizational genius resulted in ever more comprehensive information highways. First was the U.S. Postal Service, established in 1775 with Benjamin Franklin as first postmaster general. "It was by no means uncommon for merchants to send through the mail as much as $10,000 in cash," according to an essay written by Richard R. John in *A Nation Transformed by Information*. But even more important was a congressional decree mandating that newspapers be

---

[2] Alfred D. Chandler, Jr., and James W. Cortada, eds., *A Nation Transformed by Information* (Oxford University Press, 2000).

delivered by mail, subsidized in part by commercial correspondence. (In 1838 newspapers accounted for 15 percent of postal revenue, but 95 percent by weight.)

Next came the railroads, a powerful combination of new technology and private risk capital. From 1847 to 1860, track mileage grew from less than 5,000 to more than 30,000. Railroad cars replaced the stagecoach and its formidable network of roads as mail carrier of record, and for 80 years long-distance mail was sorted inside moving trains.

Samuel F.B. Morse's invention of the telegraph in 1844 spawned both the futures markets and the Associated Press and became another essential grid. A little later came Alexander Graham Bell's telephone in 1876. Then came the radio, and finally, television.

In every instance, what shines through *A Nation Transformed by Information* is the favorable climate in this country, largely nourished by the federal government working hand in hand with private industry, that made such a phenomenon possible.

A CAPSULE HISTORY OF THE INTERNET

There are several meaty capsule histories of the Internet, written by such diverse interested parties as the late science fiction author Philip K. Dick, computer science professor David Marshall at Cardiff (Wales) University, publisher and computer scientist Gregory Gromov, and computer engineer Robert H. Zakon, among others. What follows is an amalgam that combines some of the more nontechnical material from these chroniclers with data from additional sources. We pick up the timeline at 1962, just after the launch of Sputnik and the U.S. response that followed.

1962	**Packet-Switching Networks Developed**
to	The Internet transfers data in tiny packets that can
1968	take different routes to a destination. This ensures

The First Log-In—Almost

The plan to link the four ARPANET computers was unprecedented: Leonard Kleinrock, a pioneering computer science professor at UCLA, and his small group of graduate students hoped to log on to the Stanford computer and try to send it some data. They would start by typing "login" and seeing if the letters appeared on a far-off monitor.

"We set up a telephone connection between us and the guys at Stanford Research Institute," Kleinrock said in an interview. "We typed the 'L' and asked on the phone; 'Do you see the 'L'?'"

"Yes, we see the 'L,'" came the response.

"We typed the 'O' and asked, 'Do you see the 'O'?'"

"Yes, we see the 'O.'"

"Then we typed the 'G,' and the system crashed!"

But on the second attempt it worked fine, and a revolution had begun.

—The *Sacramento Bee*
May 1, 1996

both security and survival in the event of large-scale destruction such as a nuclear attack.

1969 **Birth of the Internet**
The first ARPANET mini-network is established, connecting computers at UCLA (Los Angeles), UCSB (Santa Barbara), Stanford Research Institute (Palo Alto), and the University of Utah.

1970 **First Cross-Country Link Installed by AT&T and BBN**
In 1969, computer company Bolt, Beranek and Newman from Cambridge, Massachusetts, won the contract to design and implement ARPANET. The following year they established the first transnational link from UCLA to Cambridge.

1971	**First E-Mail Applications Developed for ARPANET** Ray Tomlinson (who also gave us the @ symbol in e-mail addresses) develops the applications SNDMSG, for transmitting outgoing mail, and READMAIL, for reading incoming messages.
1973	**Global Networking Becomes a Reality** First international connections to the ARPANET are established between England (University College of London) and Norway (Royal Radar Establishment).
1976	**Networking Arrives** The same year Unix is developed (the main operating system used by universities and research establishments), Queen Elizabeth sends her first e-mail message, from the Royal Signals and Radar Establishment in Malvern, England.
1977	**E-Mail Takes Off; Internet Becomes a Reality** TheoryNet, created at the University of Wisconsin, provides electronic mail to more than 100 computer science researchers using a locally developed system.
1979	**News Groups Are Born** Usenet is developed—and still thrives today. Through MUD (Multi-User Dungeon), interactive adventure games are born.
1980	**First Internal Connections Between Files** Tim Berners-Lee, an English physicist, creates a program that makes possible the forging of internal connections between files on a network. He calls it Enquire-Within-Upon-Everything, or just plain ENQUIRE.
1984	**Domain Name System (DNS) Introduced** Number of hosts breaks 1000. Moderated newsgroups are introduced on Usenet.

> ## Why E-Mail Is Important
>
> *E-mail is a push technology: Recipients don't have to work to get it.*
> - **Pull technology.** Pull technologies require the user to actively go and retrieve the information. A book library, the Internet, and Usenet are pull technologies, requiring active and conscious participation of a human being to retrieve the information.
> - **Push technology.** Push technologies deliver information to the user, and all the user has to do is sit back and receive it. Radio, television, and e-mail are push technologies. Because push technologies are so easy to use, they get used more often. E-mail is used more than any other Internet application, even the Web.
>
> —LivingInternet.com

1986 **Transition Channel Established**
The National Science Foundation (NSF) establishes NSFNet to serve as the primary transmission channel for educational institutions, government offices, military bases, and research laboratories.

1990 **Internet Growth Explosion**
Number of hosts reaches 300,000.
ARPANET ceases operations.
The World, first commercial provider of Internet dial-up access, comes online.

1991 **Modernization Begins**
World Wide Web (the universe of network-accessible information) is developed in text-only form by Tim Berners-Lee.
WWW becomes universally accessible thanks to Gopher, an application for locating and retrieving information developed at the University of Minnesota.

1993　**WWW Revolution Begins**
The Mosaic Web browser, which adds graphics to the WWW, is developed at the University of Illinois by a team of computer scientists and students led by undergraduate Marc Andreessen.

The U.S. White House and the United Nations come online.

Number of computers with WWW access reaches 2 million.

Mosaic develops into Netscape, the most popular WWW browser to date.

America Online opens its private e-mail service to the Internet.

1994　**Commercialization Comes to the Internet**
Shopping malls and banks arrive on the Internet.

The first pizza is ordered online, from Pizza Hut.

Local communities begin to be wired directly to the Internet.

First banner ads (for Zima malt beverage) appear on hotwired.com.

Arizona law firm spams Internet with e-mail ads for green card lottery services.

1995　**Internet Goes Public**
The NSF hands control of the Internet to commercial enterprises.

1996　**Commercialization Expands**
Microsoft releases Internet Explorer, ushering in a new age of software development, with new releases being made quarterly. The "Browser Wars" officially begin.

For the first time, more e-mail than postal mail is sent in the United States.

THE INTERNET: WHERE IT'S GOING AND HOW IT GOT HERE

Marc Andreessen's Five Internet Principles to Count On

1. *Small teams work best.* Even in big companies, the best way to take advantage of Internet opportunities is to put 50 people on a project instead of 3500. Vital software is therefore developed quickly, crisply, and with tight focus. Also, spending will be in line with realistic revenue prospects.

2. *The Net allows companies to get closer to their customers.* Both negative and positive feedback arrives in real time. Ad hoc testing of new market concepts becomes practically unlimited. It is imperative for companies to put knowledge to work fast because if they don't, their customers will.

3. *Information travels faster than ever.* This applies to both news events and rumors: Consider the way the stock market fluctuates in response to new data. But it also applies to software—witness Napster. The implications of this kind of change are jarring but ultimately will be beneficial.

4. *Open systems become a lot more appealing than previously.* With the Internet it is possible to have the whole world debugging your software, suggesting new products, or providing customer service. This creates an intriguing alternative to big, centrally run companies that do their development in secret and share only the finished product with the outside world.

5. *E-mail remains the Internet's killer app.* It's simple and unglamorous, but e-mail meets a critical set of human needs. In business settings, it lets people communicate quickly, efficiently, and cheaply—whenever they want to. The social implications of enabling so many people to be a mere e-mail address away from one another continue to grow.

—*Fast Company*
February 2001

1998	**Global Expansion**
	France conducts La Fête de l'Internet, a countrywide Web fest.
	U.S. Postal Service approves electronic stamps, purchased and downloaded for printing on the Web.
	Chinese government jails Lin Hai for 2 years; the offense: providing 30,000 e-mail addresses to a U.S. Internet magazine.
1999	**Global Expansion, Continued**
	The First Internet Bank of Indiana opens on February 22 as just that: the first full-service bank available only on the Net.
2000	**More Peaks, Some Valleys**
	The dreaded Y2K bug fails to disrupt the Internet—or the rest of society—perhaps because the second millennium would not actually take place until 2001.
	First anniversary of the first full-service bank available only on the Net: The First Internet Bank of Indiana.
	On March 28, Stephen King releases his novel *Riding the Bullet* in digital form exclusively via the Web.
	Napster, e-magazines, sued for stealing intellectual property rights from musicians, composers, and writers.
	In October, the number of Internet sites reaches 22,282,727.
	Record number of dot-com start-ups fail.
2001	**The Flux Continues**
	Napster loses rights to distribute free music.
	Internet and brick-and-mortar layoffs increase.
	Mosaic architect Marc Andreessen resurfaces by cofounding Loudcloud, Inc. (www.loudcloud.com), an infrastructure service provider.

PC sales plummet due to weakening U.S. economy.

2002 **(Fill in the Blanks)**

_____
_____
_____
_____

So here we all are on the ground floor. Do we wait for the elevator, or should we walk?

CHAPTER TWO

A Web in Full: Interconnected Companies, Overlapping Interests

Way back when the Web was young—10 years or so ago—an Internet company was likely to specialize in a single service or function. Portals were portals; networks did nothing but serve as hubs connecting familial entities; search engines chugged along doing what they did best; and digital architecture firms took care of some of the infrastructure.

Today's Internet company is more likely to be a conglomerate, or at least to traffic in more than one activity. In wireless and portal environments, to mention two at random, diversification means being able to serve not only a wider range of potential clients but a larger percentage of existing clients' needs.

When six Stanford grads brainstormed over burritos in a Redwood City taco house back in February 1993, for example, all they knew for sure was that they didn't want to work for a big company. What they came up with less than a year later (holding down day jobs to pay the rent) was Excite.com, a software product that combined search-and-retrieval with automatic hypertext linking. In just one more year, Excite had become a leading Web portal, offering free, personalized services, state-of-the-art search technology, and 18 programmed channels of content.

Unfortunately, those of the six partners still with the firm accomplished only part of their objective: In spite of themselves, they all now work for a large company. Then again, that doesn't seem so important to them today. In 1999, Excite.com joined forces with @Home Network, an aggressive communications company whose principal priority was to harness a variety of forms of advanced technology. It had done this so well that it was able to offer connections up to a hundred times faster than traditional telephone modems. The resulting new media powerhouse, Excite@Home, can provide both home and business customers with 24-hour access to advanced, personalized services over such communications devices as PCs, pagers, cellular phones, and television sets. It offers interactive content developed by more than 100 programming affiliates, including CNN, Fox, MSNBC, the *New York Times*, and *USA Today*. Not quite of AOL–Time Warner proportions, but formidable indeed.

Mirroring the vagaries of the Internet itself, Excite@Home's progress has suffered its own hiccups. Its broadband technology—provided by the "@Home" part of the company—still remains years away from replacing phone modems for Internet access, which has put the company's stock in a nosedive and precipitated two layoffs between January and June of 2001. It may take some time for the high-speed cable connections offered by Excite@Home, Verizon, and AT&T to make their mark. Unfortunately, in this group (plus a number of other competitors) only Excite@Home has so much at stake.

NATURAL PARTNERS

Sometimes the fit between two parallel products or services is so close as to be a natural. K.C. Donovan, a vice president at Globix Corporation, has seen this occur in companies offering Internet service provider (ISP) hosting or co-location services.

"Web hosting, which is what we do," says Donovan, "consists of giving clients the content of what they want sent to the Internet and then

A WEB IN FULL: INTERCONNECTED COMPANIES, OVERLAPPING INTERESTS

> ### The Net as a Village
>
> Even though the Internet is a global network, in many ways it resembles a small town with similar services. If you want to send or receive mail, the Internet has electronic post offices. There are online libraries you can use all day or night, with millions of books and periodicals for unlimited browsing. Chat rooms serve as 24-hour Internet coffeehouses, with people eager to gab anytime you want. You can shop, order a pizza, preview a movie, and listen to radio stations from all over the world.
>
> Many different kinds of communication go on at the same time. You use different software programs to complete different tasks, such as a Web browser to access shopping sites and an e-mail program to send and receive messages.
>
> Some programs are able to offer more than one service. Netscape Communicator, for example, has a Web browser (called Netscape Navigator), an e-mail program, and a newsreader. You can also use more specialized software, such as the stand-alone e-mail program Eudora, or combine different software packages into a system that works for you.
>
> —Copyright © 1996–2001
> Michael Lerner Productions
> www.learnthenet.com

placing that content on the company's server for use, ultimately, anywhere in the world. Co-location specialists invite clients to store equipment at a facility made available by the co-location company, and even provide a network to tie into. Exodus Communications now does both, for example. They started in co-location and recognized after a while that they could do Web hosting as well. It offered them a quick way to reach another market synergistically.

"Over the past year we've seen some of the better-funded companies, like Intel for example, recognizing that there is money to be made in the data center business. So they got into that as well. A combination of large companies with deep pockets gets into new industries where they see opportunities that fit their product lines. There are also companies with less money but with good ideas being gobbled up by midsized companies."

WHEN BUSINESS MARRIAGES GO BAD

U.S. mergers and acquisitions in the 1990s numbered roughly 46,000, with a value of some $4.8 trillion. But a study by the consulting firm A.T. Kearney and the *Chicago Tribune* found 7 out of 10 of the merged companies lagging behind their peers in sales, profit growth, and underperforming stocks.

Big losers were the tens of thousands of workers whose jobs were eliminated, especially older workers, women, and minorities, who disproportionately carry the biggest burden, according to government figures. Customers also lose, often suffering through service interruptions. Communities lose part of their fabric when doors close on businesses that pay for their infrastructure with taxes.

A typical example is the DaimlerChrysler deal, thought to be a natural fit between two equal partners. As Daimler pursued Chrysler, it paid too little attention to the financial situation, according to former Chrysler executive Gerald Greenwald. "Anytime you hear 'merger of equals,' run the other way," he said. "Acquirers anxious to get the deal done will often make promises or overlook potential trouble spots during due diligence."

The biggest Internet-media merger, America Online–Time Warner, took a year to be consummated after its announcement in January 2000. More than a year later, this $160 billion blockbuster was still sorting itself out. The merged company set aggressive targets for growth and fared better in the 2001 economic downturn than most Internet companies. Still, thousands of employees lost jobs during the shakedown period, and AOL's stock drop of nearly 50 percent at about the time the deal was disclosed sharply cut the merger's value.

A WEB IN FULL: INTERCONNECTED COMPANIES, OVERLAPPING INTERESTS

> **Dot-Com Legal Guidance—Lawyer Optional**
>
> "Being confident how you approach negotiations and deal-making is everything in this business," said Amandilo Cousin, vice president of a six-person Hollywood talent agency. "But we felt at a disadvantage in contract negotiations because we couldn't afford the high-priced legal advice."
>
> Enter LawVantage.com, a site Mr. Cousin found on the Internet that offered a library of documents he could use as frameworks. Instead of hiring lawyers to draft contracts at thousands of dollars a day, he took the generic documents to lawyers who customized them for several hundred dollars apiece.
>
> LawVantage.com is one of several Web sites that have sprung up to offer legal services. As a result, analysts say, the industry may be on the verge of fundamental changes—charging by the service instead of by the hour. As online services grow, say the experts, the reduced demand for traditional services could force lawyers to lower fees.
>
> —Jennifer S. Lee
> Adapted from the *New York Times*

INDUSTRY BREAKDOWN

It still is possible to differentiate among the different kinds of Internet companies, although in another decade the water may be even muddier than it is today. There are a number of ways to carve up the variegated categories of goods, services, and specialties out there. One useful breakdown is adapted from *The WetFeet.com Insider Guide, Version 2000*. In addition to e-commerce, which will be covered in Chapter 3, there are:

- *Media*. On the Internet the term *media* covers a wide range, from online publications that try to make money by selling advertising or subscriptions to companies like RealNetworks that create software that helps bring media to life on the Internet. On the publication side, there are both online ventures of traditional media companies, like New York Times Interactive, and pure online plays, like the financial site TheStreet.com. Other niche media sites include JollyRoger.com (see Chapter 3), the short film and animation company Atom Films, and the online music company Listen.com. Service providers such as AOL, and portals such as Yahoo, also see themselves as media companies—which is one reason AOL purchased Time Warner.

- *Portals*. Accounting for some of the busiest Web sites, portals are aggregators. They provide a huge number of links to other Web sites and businesses and are designed to serve as a home base for Web surfers. These sites make their money from advertising and through alliances with companies that pay for the privilege of serving as the aggregator's preferred provider of travel services, greeting cards, or whatever. Today, portals offer a wide array of services, including e-mail, shopping, news, and community. Major portals include Yahoo, Excite@Home (see Chapter 2), Lycos, and LookSmart.
- *Internet services*. In this context, Internet services encompass all the companies that support and enable the Internet. Included are ISPs like Earthlink that help companies and individuals get on the Web, consulting firms like Equient (see Chapter 3) that help companies design and develop e-businesses, and online corporate communication companies like Corporate Technology Communications (see Chapter 1).
- *Internet infrastructure*. Many companies build the infrastructure necessary to create and maintain a Web site. Globix, for example, operates its own fiber-optic backbone and hosts companies' Web servers (see Chapter 2). Enterasys (see Chapter 2) provides infrastructure solutions for enterprise customers. Oracle creates databases for Internet companies. Broadcom creates circuits that enable data, video, and other broadband communication.

Inside View

Ron Gula, Vice President, Intrusion Detection Products, Enterasys

Enterasys Networks (http://www.enterasys.com) develops equipment that aids companies in running secure, scalable networks. The intrusion detection arm of Enterasys is run by Ron Gula, who has been fascinated with the security aspects of the Internet since his college days, and who created a security company specifically to be acquired by a larger corporation.

Q How did you get into this business?
A I guess I've always been into computers and security, even though I don't have a hacker background.

Q Where did you develop your interest?
A Mostly from being exposed to the Internet. I don't know if you were on the Internet in the late eighties, but there were things like the Gopher system, where you could FTP (File Transfer Protocol) into certain places and get text files on almost anything, from recipes to reasons why the Lochness monster is alive. In all that noise was a certain area of security, whether it was phone systems, alarm systems, or computer systems.

I describe myself as a systems engineer. The neat thing about security is that there is a way to take a complex system, find a path through all the components, and violate the security model of the system. This is all very addictive to me.

Q So how did you finally begin to apply your interest?
A I was at a company in Annapolis, Maryland, using an instrument called intrusion detection—which is a bit like radar for hackers—and felt that I could do a better job than they were doing. I left the company and founded my own. It was called Network Security Wizards. I designed the company to be very light on management and very heavy on technical expertise. Actually, I designed the company as an acquisitions candidate.

continued on next page

Q   You sold the company to Enterasys then?
A   Absolutely. There was a merger in September 2000. As with all acquisitions and mergers, there's a certain period of getting all the books in order, but we've been progressing very well.

Q   How many people did you bring along with you?
A   Thirteen. Actually, during the acquisition we were more like six or seven people. Since then we've been going through Enterasys, sprinkling our brand of security in the various training and sales support areas to the point where we have about 300 people out of 2000 who know the basics of security really well.

Q   How would you describe your basic purpose?
A   We're in the business of catching thieves. It's not just move and countermove, attack and counterattack. We do a lot of that, of course, but we also determine the generalities that viruses have in common and how to detect them. In other words, we don't concentrate on viruses, we concentrate on hacker techniques.

Q   And each client has its own problem.
A   No question. One of the reasons we've been successful is that the latest tendencies of the hacker are embodied in our product. If a client wanted to take our system and do analyses for abuse on the job (employees playing games, trading stock, gambling, downloading pornography, and the like), our product can do that. Other clients focus on more sophisticated business problems such as verifying that all of their routers are operating correctly and in an appropriate manner.

A specific example: Most of the products that exist on the market today can look at only small amounts of data. A T1 line, for example, consists of 1.544 megabits a second worth of data. A large high school would use a T1 for its local area network (LAN). A major university with 50,000 students may need two or three T3s, each of which contains 28 T1 lines. Our product can monitor three T3s with just one box. Most of our competitors would require 5 to 10 boxes.

continued on next page

> Q What do the people who work for you need to be good at?
> A I'm very traditional when it comes to software development. You have engineers build stuff, your researchers do the heavy thinking, a group of people do quality control, and a customer service group provides support. Whether you're Microsoft or IBM, these are the four functions of software development.
>
> The paradox here is that part of being a security expert is being a generalist. Most of our folks are by nature jacks of all trades and experts in maybe one or two. You may not be able to code Java, but you have to know that there are 10 things you should look out for when you download a Java applet. You may not be able to program in assembly code for an IBM VMS system, but if you're looking at network traffic you still have to recognize an attack that's written in VMS.
>
> Q Where would I go to learn those basics?
> A The Sans Institute (http://www.sans.institute.org) offers a certification course, among others. FoundStone (http://www.foundstone.com) has a variety of training courses and is getting some good press now. Ernst & Young (http://www.cgey.com/index.shtml) offers a course called Extreme Hacking. If you're interested in the basics, these three sources offer a good cross section.

THE SPIDERWEB EFFECT

Companies will continue to slough off their least profitable product and service lines, and will add others they hope (but only after exhaustive research, ahem) will do better. The composition and direction of each new acquisition or enterprise will depend on the company's perception of the market niche(s) being staked out, as well as the shifting needs of the clients and customers being served.

But any business strategy is worthless if management can't deliver on its promises.

Executives must be flexible enough to anticipate problems and solve them quickly. Any company without the capacity to build momentum will slide backward—fast.

And this is one of the areas in which you will be counted on to help keep things moving forward at your company.

CHAPTER THREE

E-Commerce Companies: Life on the Edge

Electronic commerce, e-commerce, e-tailing, B2B, B-to-C. Whatever the label, these are terms used to describe any business transaction via the Internet. Defining electronic business is the easy part, though. Attempting to put its future in sharp focus is somewhat more difficult. This is largely because we now have entered the arcane world of statistics, and everyone knows that statisticians can work miracles with numbers—and also that their interpretations often depend on the needs of their clients. But even independent researchers' survey results can vary wildly.

Let's start, then, with the numbers. According to eMarketer.com ("the world's leading provider of Internet statistics"), worldwide e-commerce revenues are expected to more than triple from $381 billion in 2001 to $1.24 trillion in 2003. Other researchers come to other conclusions, both above and below eMarketer's—one as high as $3.2 trillion. So we'll see. During this period, U.S. e-commerce dominance is expected to fall from a little under three-fourths to a little over one-half of all Internet business conducted worldwide—or about $650 billion.

BUSINESS-TO-CONSUMER BUSINESS

Online shopping is the central focus of e-commerce today. In this country, auction site eBay and the megabookstore Amazon.com, both of which conduct 100 percent of their business online, are two of many e-commerce companies that qualify as dot-coms, also called *pure-plays*. Home Depot and Wal-Mart, which offer goods both online and in physical stores, were the top-ranked clicks-and-mortar companies (in combined in-store and online revenues) early in 2001.

A few years ago this distinction was much clearer, when the Internet was filled with companies whose only business was online business. Two of them, eToys and Buy.com, were thought to be models of successful start-ups. eToys became a highly visible brand with a well-designed Web site and highly efficient warehousing and fulfillment operations. Buy.com took a different path, selling products below cost to attract bargain hunters and adding revenue by accepting advertising. Then came executive decisions that would haunt both companies. eToys expanded so rapidly that it went deeply into debt—$280 million worth. It also turned down potentially lucrative affiliations with Wal-Mart and Toys-R-Us. Buy.com, however, was too late in realizing that to make a profit it had to charge more for its products than it paid for them.

The result? When eToys 2000 holiday sales came in at half its projections, its death was assured. On March 1, 2001, after failing to find a buyer, the company shut down for good, with stockholders unlikely ever to see a dime. (Stock had fallen to 9 cents a share—from a high of $84.25 in 1999—before trading was halted on the Nasdaq stock market.) At about the same time, Buy.com was scrambling for survival. While it did crawl closer to profitability by increasing prices, it also lost many of its core, discount-hunting customers. Buy.com's holiday sales also were off the mark—so far off that it was forced to fold both its Canadian and British operations. After firing its two top executives and laying off 40 percent of its 230 full-time employees, Buy.com's stock fell from a high of $27.50 per share in 2000 to 41 cents.

> ### Safe E-Commerce?
>
> "The idea of my credit card being 'safe' is by and large a myth," says Farhad Mohit, president and CEO of BizRate.com, a company that rates online shopping sites. "Everybody in the business, everybody who understands encryption methodology, knows that if I want to steal credit card numbers, I ask you which is easier: to pay $100 to a busboy in a restaurant and have him give me a bunch of them every night, or to set up a computer science geek with a minicomputer and encryption-breaking technology to try and get a credit card? There's no contest."
>
> —Kyle Schurman
> *Smart Computing*

In the spring of 2001, the company's future was very much in doubt. First-quarter revenues for 2001 fell 40 percent, from $208 million to $125 million.

But wait. Somebody nearby must know a corporate adaptation of the Heimlich maneuver. Almost at the same time Buy.com's gloomy revenue results were publicized on May 2, the company announced a 58 percent increase in customer accounts over the previous year. Two weeks later it consummated a joint venture with Motorola that could expand exponentially the company's wireless messaging services. At about that same time came the icing, in the form of a *Forbes* magazine award naming Buy.com "Best of the Web" for the second consecutive year in the computer and electronics category. It was obvious—there in the middle of 2001, anyway—that Buy.com was still kicking.

During that same period, in the "real world" of stores and doors, it was business as usual. Shoppers saw, heard, smelled, or felt products that interested them, made their choices, stood in line, and carried home their booty. Home Depot and Wal-Mart, each with a net income in the billions in 2000, managed to record just over 1 percent of their totals, respectively, through online revenues.

> ### The Freebie Is Dead
>
> For a couple of years late last century, consumers could go online and get practically anything for free. With too much money chasing too few customers, companies ladled out CDs, MP3s, PCs, and DVDs. Drugstore.com scattered handfuls of free shampoo and toothpaste with nominal purchases. Health and beauty retailer More.com let customers lock in prices "for life."
>
> But when More.com was purchased by Health Central, new COO Fred Toney saw things a bit differently: "These outrageous discounts don't work in the offline world, and they don't work in the online world," he said. "We've seen a lot of companies go away because of promotions that didn't make a lot of sense."
>
> The handwriting is on the wall. Napster retooled itself to charge for services, and MP3.com rolled out fees for music storage, and neither of them made it, although not just for those reasons. It's looking more and more as though in today's Internet economy, you'll get what you pay for.
>
> —Adapted from *The Standard*

"We're still shifting toward an Internet economy," says Richard Johnson, president of New York–based HotJobs.com. "The brick-and-mortars have learned their lessons—from both successes and failures—and the next wave of Internet development will come from traditional companies."

Paul Rand, president and founder of Corporate Technology Communications, believes that eventually the "e-" prefix used with most Internet-related descriptors will disappear. "E-commerce and e-mail will become simply "mail" and "commerce," says Rand. "And where the question used to be 'What is your Internet strategy?' it will become 'What's your overall business strategy?'—with the Internet, of course, being an integral component. And the convergence of all these different technologies into the mainstream of business applications is where the market is headed. Increasingly, companies looking at technology as a tool and medium for

> **Sock Puppet Survives**
>
> In November 2000, Pets.com let go 255 of its 320 employees. The remaining 65 stayed on to sell off the company's assets. Unfortunately, its $18.2 million in prepaid advertising was a complete write-off. It got little for the $7.8 million in inventory on its books, but did donate 21 tons of dog food to feed starving Alaskan sled dogs. Pets.com's best asset turned out to be its Sock Puppet icon. *Me By Me*, the Sock Puppet's autobiography, immediately rocketed onto Amazon.com's list of best-selling titles.
>
> —Owen Thomas
> Adapted from *ecompany.com*

growing their businesses—rather than the business as an end in itself—are the ones that are going to thrive."

STAY SMALL TO SURVIVE

It may be that modest ambition is one key to survival. Both huge pure-play companies mentioned earlier, Amazon.com and eBay, were in trouble early in 2001. Amazon.com's working capital (current assets minus current liabilities) has dropped steadily every quarter since the beginning of 2000 and was projected to go in the red before the end of 2002—about the same time it hoped to turn its first profit. One problem was that to reach profitability it had to abandon the discount policy that had attracted large numbers of bargain-book hunters. (Meanwhile, small booksellers that have held on are seeing an increase in business. Terence McCoy, co-owner of St. Mark's Bookshop in New York City, told the *New York Times*, "I knew that they'd have to stop eventually if they had to show a profit. At some point they can't discount. It's fairly simple arithmetic.")

Giant eBay, with 90 percent of consumer revenues in the auction market, was financially secure but had been plagued with technical problems for 3 successive years. One 1999 crash caused the site to disappear for a record 22 hours.

Back at the other end of the spectrum, hundreds of smaller dot-coms—many with 25 employees or fewer—are plodding along, slowly but steadily, learning as they go but being careful not to overreach. Avoiding lavish product-launch parties and Super Bowl commercials, they expand only when they can afford to. They concentrate on keeping costs down, revenues up, and, most important, turning shoppers into buyers. A survey by Chicago outplacement firm Challenger, Gray & Christmas put the number of lost U.S. dot-com jobs at 16,000 for the 3 months ending February 2001. The U.S. Bureau of Labor Statistics, however, estimated that 11,000 Internet jobs were created during the same period.

The Internet Got Me Decent Football Seats

"When Northwestern, my alma mater, recently played in the Alamo Bowl, I ordered tickets through the school's athletic department. When I got them, I almost burned down my apartment in anger. The seats were deep in the end zone of a stadium with short sight lines. I was stuck with incredibly crummy seats!

"Now in the old world I'd have to buy ridiculously priced tickets from a scalper if I wanted to really see the game. Fortunately, we live in the electronic age. I got on the computer. First stop: the Alamo Bowl's Web site, which took me to Ticketmaster. There, available at face value, was a seat on the 35-yard line, five rows beneath the press box on the Northwestern side. The transaction took 10 minutes.

"When I got to the will-call window at the Alamodome, there was a line of people who had similarly ventured online to improve their seats. None of us was forced to haggle over price with some bottom-feeding ticket reseller. Isn't e-commerce supposed to be about efficient, value-added transactions? That's what I had."

—Todd Allen, www.chicagobraintrust.com
Adapted from the *Chicago Tribune*

Inside View

Dr. Elliot McGucken, Founder and President, JollyRoger.com

In 1999, Elliot McGucken quit a job teaching physics at Davidson College to maintain full-time the 24 Web sites he had created and developed. Most of these sites are devoted to classical literature, and so far they're making money. Elliot's print-on-demand novel, The Tragedy of Drake Raft.com, was the number-one-selling book in North Carolina at Amazon.com last September. "Moby Dick," a documentary he shot with one of his friends, reflects his ardent interest in nineteenth-century novelist Herman Melville. For these and other reasons, Elliot has been called a Renaissance man.

Q It sounds as though you're enjoying yourself.
A Yes, this is a good time. I kind of stumbled on it 5 years ago.

Q Are you currently a one-man band?
A Yes. I never really went the venture-capital route. As soon as you raise VC you have to worry about things like hiring people. After talking to other site owners, I could tell that before long my job would be more about managing people than running the site.

Q You don't even have a high school kid to help you with your databases or electronic filing?
A No, the whole trick is to think of software as a machine, as a kind of labor-saving device. Ten years ago if you wanted to get something out to 30,000 people, you'd have to fold it and stamp it and put it in the mail. Now we have the software and the hardware infrastructure that replaces all that labor. So I see it as a tool that delivers information. When you think about it, software is labor "immortalized." In software, words and thoughts become actions. One person can deliver information to 30,000 people all over the world—at a very low cost. It's a brand-new paradigm that happened so quickly. Yet we take it for granted now.

continued on next page

THE DOT-COM LANDSCAPE: A VIEW FROM THE INSIDE

Q Twenty-four Web sites—you have a lot going on.
A Well, in the classics space all your best employees are already dead. They created some of the greatest content ever, and we get to use it. At JollyRoger.com, you can leverage Einstein's work, you can leverage Dostoyevsky's work, you can leverage William Faulkner's work.

By the way, the classics are *entertainment* immortalized. Software is also an open source. I don't really pay for the content. Come to think of it, you can leverage Bill Gates, too. I often think I got a better deal from Microsoft than they got from me. I paid them a couple hundred dollars, but they've saved me a whole lot more over the years. I don't pay for the operating system, either. I use Red Hat Linux,[1] and there's just so much out there you can leverage for free. JollyRoger.com basically consists of marrying immortal labor to immortal entertainment.

Q Did you abandon Windows and go Linux all the way?
A I use Windows on my desktop for word processing and some day-to-day applications. But I've always used Linux for my servers. One of my Linux servers has been running for 2 years without ever being restarted.

Q So your revenues come largely from advertising. Do you work with an agency?
A Yes, a couple of them. For a while the split was 70 percent for me and 30 for them. But they've just changed it 50 to 50.

Q That's a pretty big bite compared to agency fees in the brick-and-mortar world. Is that going to work for you?
A Well, I have nonexclusive agreements, so I have to see what is selling and move the ads around according to who is paying me the most. And the volume will have to go up, obviously. But 2 years ago I was making $3,000 a month, and today I'm making $6,000. No matter how small your Web site is, you can start earning revenue. You can

---

[1] Red Hat Linux: version of an operating system whose source code is freely available to everyone—in contrast to Windows, for example.

continued on next page

even partner—like in a co-op. If you join CommissionJunction.com (http://www.cj.com), for example, you can partner with more than a thousand other merchants such as Amazon.com (through their affiliates program), Barnes&Noble.com, and Excite@Home.

Q   Was there a flash point during the time you were teaching when you said, "I'd like to do this full-time"?
A   I always said I *wasn't* going to do this full-time. But I also always liked writing, and for me this has turned out to be a new way of writing—just in a different medium.

Q   What do you like most about what you do?
A   JollyRoger.com is a place where anyone can get on and be an expert. I have well over 1000 discussion groups going on, featuring just about everyone you can think of. The first four listed currently are Gabriel Garcia Marquez, *Beowulf*, Harry Potter, and Shakespeare, followed, by the way, by a "Heavyweight Title Bout—God v. Atheists: Atheists v. God." Now that's diverse! [To find Jolly Roger, point your browser to http://jollyroger.com.]

ONLINE PUBLISHING

Most of the attention going to e-books has centered in the past couple of years on relatively dramatic phenomena. One was Stephen King's novel *Riding the Bullet*, bought by 500,000 Web surfers after exclusive Internet publication in March 2000. Another was the development of books designed to be read on handheld wireless devices rather than between covers. (To turn page, hit Enter.) The electronic version of vanity publishing has lured thousands of unpublished writers to spend $1500 or more to access a process they are assured will bring them instant fame.

In 2001, electronic publishing reached the mainstream. At a Jupiter Research media forum held in New York City in March, Time Warner's chairman of trade publishing cited the need for lower-priced e-books and the concomitant benefits of building an in-house digital structure. At about the same time, media giant Thomson Corporation announced that electronic products and services accounted for 53 percent ($3.15 billion) of its total revenues the previous year. Thomson's learning group, in turn, recorded the largest corporate sales gain that year—40.4 percent, to $1.39 billion.

Educational publishing is coming to the dot-coms as well. OpenMind Publishing Group, one of several e-publishers specializing in higher education, was founded in 2000 by Paul Elliot and Brad Schultz, two former McGraw-Hill College Division sales and marketing executives.

"We realized that our customers—by which I mean professors and students—weren't buying what the traditional publishing world was selling," says Elliot. "We saw a lot of dissatisfaction. Even when a professor assigned a textbook, a third of the students wouldn't buy it. Ten percent or more shared the materials, and another 20 percent just tried to get by with lecture notes.

"So professors and students are both actively seeking alternatives to what traditional publishers are offering. And the answer, we felt, was to

Harry Potter, Web Developer

After an abortive online liaison with AOL in 1993, educational publisher Scholastic tried and abandoned several Internet strategies, and maintained a sporadic Net presence at best. But that was before the company bid successfully in 1998 for the rights to Harry Potter, the children's book series about a boy wizard. The series' sales helped boost Scholastic's annual revenues to $1.4 billion in 2000, which made a $22 million Web site suddenly affordable. Not that Scholastic was being accused of a whimsical impulse purchase. The site's teachers' section recorded 453,000 unique visitors in 2000 (up 600 percent from 1999); visits to the kids' section rose to 792,000.

—Lisa Shuchman
Adapted from *The Industry Standard*

personalize the content. There is some market reluctance in the acceptance of trade e-books, but this isn't the case with textbooks. Our toughest problem was how to deal with the authors whose work would be changed almost to the point of being unrecognizable.

"I was enrolled in an executive MBA program at Wake Forest at the time and was exposed to the open source movement through a Linux project I was doing for Red Hat. I saw that this relatively informal process had real crossover possibilities, particularly in such academic concepts as peer review and knowledge sharing. Professors, by the way, intuitively understand this concept—it's the way they live their lives. So we looked at these concepts in a slightly different way and decided we could apply them to baseline textbook content."

The Cary, North Carolina–based company (www.ompg.com) started with the introductory markets—government, economics, political science—because that content is more generic, and the classes the largest. This decision also posed the fewest copyright problems, dealing as it did with authors more likely to share their intellectual capital with others in a collaborative publishing process.

"There's a parallel we can draw with custom publishing," says Paul Elliot, "which 5 or 6 years ago consisted of individuals creating all of their materials in a non-networked world. Today in a networked world we have the capacity to share. This was our one similarity with Napster, by the way, until they were put out of business. The big difference between OpenMind and Napster, of course, is that they used material somebody else owned, whereas we own the material we allow people to use. Then once somebody makes any changes—if they choose to share them with the community—there's an unlimited commercial use license available to everybody in that community.

"We have an American government book to which we have allowed professors to make radical changes to accommodate their particular curricula. One professor is weaving an African-American perspective throughout the book, for example. So we end up with a completely different product. It cost us virtually nothing for the professor to republish his own mix—and it exponentially expands our market potential. The best part is that we can offer textbooks to students for 70 percent less than they would pay in bookstores."

As of spring 2001, more than 8000 professors had registered with OpenMind, double the number on board just 2 months earlier. Dr. Martin Starr, a professor of production and operations management for graduate students at Rollins College's Crummer Business School, was one of the first authors to sign on. Dr. Starr considers OpenMind a progressive oasis in what he believes is an increasingly hostile industry for authors.

"My original book came out with a small publisher in 1997," says Dr. Starr, "and was one of the company's leading texts. I had a wonderful editor with great ideas. But when time came to revise it, the company was bought out by a huge publisher. They fired my editor and shifted my book to two different divisions before deciding they had no use for it. It had been reviewed very well, but they didn't care. I decided to bring the book out in CD form, which is not only more flexible but less expensive. It also allows me to include linkages that bring an entire new dimension to the book. Some of my students helped me put it out both in PDF and HTML format. I also discovered that I could customize the book as easily as I could revise it.

"When I discovered the OpenMind people, I knew we were talking the same language. Not only that: They had a business model whereby both they and I could make money on the book almost immediately. For academics, this is really a natural." (For a complete description of Dr. Starr's work, see his Web site at www.starrpublishing.com.)

BUSINESS-TO-BUSINESS BUSINESS

Business-to-business (B2B) is where the action is going to be, so say most experts. How much action is difficult to say because we're again at the mercy of the researchers and their contradictory projections. For example, in 1998 International Data Corporation estimated that 1999 B2B worldwide sales would be $46.2 billion. Six months later they said such sales would reach $80.4 billion. Forrester Research worked out a technique to have it both ways. In the fall of 1998 they estimated that $327 billion B2B commerce would be transacted by 2002. In February 1999, they projected B2B e-commerce for 2003 at about $1.6 trillion. Since then Forrester has published both optimistic and pessimistic estimates for 2003. (Its low projection for *total* e-commerce worldwide in 2003 was $1.8 trillion; its high projection $3.2 trillion.) General advice: When reading projections, be skeptical.

Paul Larson and Jeff Fischer, of the online business investment publication *The Motley Fool.com*, describe two basically different types of B2B companies—horizontal and vertical. Vertical companies work within an industry, and typically make their money from advertising or transaction fees from the e-commerce they may host. Horizontal companies Larson and Fischer call a completely different breed, and operate at different levels across numerous different verticals. Some of them, for example, help make manufacturing processes run more efficiently; others empower sales forces with critical information.

Other reasons for increased B2B e-commerce:

- Reduced purchasing costs
- Increased market efficiency
- Greater market intelligence
- Decreased inventory levels

The overriding attraction that runs throughout online B2B is that it can make companies much more efficient. Increased efficiencies mean reduced costs, a goal that interests every company. For these reasons, as well as others, the potential for the B2B e-commerce industry in the years to come is enormous.

One transaction reflecting all of these arguments (as well as offering a powerful case for potential B2B muscle) took place between General Motors and Ford in May 2000, establishing an Internet trading exchange that would combine the two companies' supply chains. Each year the two auto giants buy a combined $80 billion in raw materials and auto parts from more than 30,000 suppliers. Their trading exchange will save billions of dollars in lower prices, transaction efficiency, and supply-chain improvements. Such transactions will create jobs. Further, perhaps some of the savings will be passed on to the consumer.

PART TWO

Dot-Com Diary: Analysis of a Start-Up

What kinds of people start Internet companies? What fuels their inspiration and drive to create a business from scratch? And what problems must entrepreneurs deal with on a daily basis to keep their businesses alive and make them grow successfully? YouKnowBest.com is a Florida start-up begun in 1999 by Rob Wight and Alan Fulmer. In Chapters 4, 5, and 6, the two founders take us through some of the crucial decisions that etched their initial vision, their financial underpinnings, and their strategy for hiring a team to help fulfill their dream.

CHAPTER FOUR

Isolating a Market Niche: Framing a Mission

At a meeting one Friday afternoon in the fall of 1998, Rob Wight, a Windows general manager at Microsoft, scribbled notes as founder and chairman Bill Gates described for a dozen or so key managers three significant areas in which he predicted the Internet would rapidly evolve. As Rob recalls from his notes, these areas would address:

- The need for differentiation as portal sites become indistinguishable from one another, offering many of the same services
- The emergence of topic-based, shopping-based, or geography-based portal sites
- The emergence of quality rating services on the Web, driven by users

This meeting and Gates's words percolated in Rob's mind for the following month, when he met with Alan Fulmer, a friend of 25 years. The two had stayed in touch since their high school days in Rochester, New York. Rob and Alan, an information technology contractor for the

American Automobile Association (AAA), had talked for years about going into business together.

THE MICROSOFT CONNECTION

What Gates had proposed at that 1998 meeting—an offhand discussion that had nothing to do with the original agenda—was the inspiration for a new way of looking at product development that Microsoft now calls .NET strategy.[1] This was intended to bring together all of the disparate forms of technology that are in one's life right now. The first initiative in the strategy, code-named Hailstorm, brings together Microsoft's Instant Messenger and its information profiling tool, Passport—and combines both with a strategic alliance involving eBay.

"Right now," says Alan Fulmer, "you have to go one place to get one thing, and another place to get another thing. You use the Internet in some situations, your telephone in others, and your television in still others. The .NET strategy was designed to bring together all of these different technologies and make them one—intended to work for one person at a time.

"We were looking down that same road of aggregation, but we specialized in decision support, or the knowledge management area. And we said, 'That's what we want to do. We want to help people make decisions.' Right now the decisions we are helping people make happen to be in the area of selecting product. But the technology we've created is one that can be used for any kind of decision-making scenario."

UNINTENDED INSPIRATION

By the end of 1998, Rob Wight had left Microsoft. Doctors told the Wights that son Alex, suffering from a serious ear infection, could be

---

[1] Hailstorm, the first stage of Microsoft's .NET strategy, was scheduled for rollout in 2001. Hailstorm is described in a series of related articles at www.techweb.com/wire/storyTWB20010118S0019, as well as at www.microsoft.com/net/hailstorm.asp.

ISOLATING A MARKET NICHE: FRAMING A MISSION

> ### EBay's New Best Friend
>
> For months investors have had their eye on eBay, wondering how the economic slowdown would affect a business that has never had to weather a slump in consumer spending. The San Jose, California, company took a high-profile step last week to assuage those concerns: It announced that it will become the first major customer of Microsoft's .NET Web services, which provide Internet-based software that is supposed to help businesses work together more smoothly. The deal helps eBay continue to draw more customers beyond its traditional consumer base in collectibles. The agreement with Microsoft means there will be links to eBay from two popular Microsoft portals—Carpoint for vehicle sales and bCentral for small businesses.
>
> The bCentral portal already lets companies automate their online sales, and eBay CEO Meg Whitman is betting that bCentral will help businesses clear the technological hurdles that have so far kept many of them off eBay.
>
> —Eric Young
> Adapted from *The Industry Standard*
> March 26, 2001

helped only if the family moved to a drier climate. The Wights chose Florida, where Alan Fulmer had lived since 1984. As the two discussed other possibilities for collaboration, another event crystallized the conception of YouKnowBest.

In December 1999, after an afternoon meeting in southern Florida, Rob and friend Otto Ritter headed home in a driving rain. Suddenly a car behind them in the adjacent lane veered toward them on the rain-slicked Florida Turnpike, clipping the rear bumper of Otto's car with its right front fender. The impact sent their car into a 360-degree spin, then onto the shoulder, where it finally came to rest against the guardrail. When they got out to inspect the damage, Otto and Rob saw the rear bumper jammed into the wheel well, but otherwise the car was without a scratch—and still drivable. Rob and Otto were shaken, but uninjured.

On impulse, Rob searched the Internet for information on car safety. What he learned was that data on buying a safe car through the Web was difficult to find, difficult to sort, and incomplete at best. If a techie had so much trouble, he concluded, chances were good that many average Internet users faced similar frustration—even if their reasons for seeking such information weren't quite as grim as Rob's had been.

In late 1999, the relationship between Internet users and the Internet itself was a relatively passive one. But as the technology improved, users became more sophisticated. New software began to noticeably improve the speed and interactive nature of Web sites. Twenty-four-hour access to the Internet through cable modems and DSL connections were increasing as well.

As users began to interact more with the Internet, Rob and Alan sensed that they also would welcome more direct involvement with what they did online. In the e-commerce sector in particular, they believed, customers were ready to take a more assertive role in the selection of vendors, products, and services—if only because they could. Internet consumers were becoming more savvy and were also looking for ways to get better and more complete information before making purchase decisions.

THE BUSINESS MODEL

"We saw that the true power of the Internet was the sharing of information," says Alan. "In the past—in the retail sector at least—this information was held closely by the merchants. Now, instead of relying on the suggestions of a single salesclerk, users could research publications, manufacturers, e-commerce stores, and the recommendations of other product users." The entire e-commerce experience, in other words, was still focused on the marketplace or on the products, rather than on the user.

But how could they provide this service free to the consumers and still make a profit? Who would pay their bills? The answer came from building relationships with three sources: vendors, manufacturers, and content providers.

Vendors

The idea was to have vendors send in feeds of data, which in turn established what products YouKnowBest ultimately displayed to people. The sequence was for a user to download the application software, decide what products are of interest, and purchase those products through the vendors. YouKnowBest gets paid a commission based on those purchases. By March 2001, 700 vendors were signed up in 20 industries, among them computing, electronics, clothing, home and garden, and sporting goods. YouKnowBest carries 3.3 million products in their database from those vendors. Commissions vary depending on the market.

Manufacturers

There are three parts to YouKnowBest's relationship with manufacturers: (1) a database of manufacturers, based on the products the vendors have provided, (2) a reference for consumers of what manufacturers make what products, and (3) a way for the manufacturers to promote their products directly and give them the opportunity to build strategic relationships with YouKnowBest.

Content Providers

A number of sites on the Internet furnish information ("provide content") about products and offer product information, reviews, and advice. The content providers act as a sales force for YouKnowBest. Their identities are placed on the YouKnowBest site, which is linked to them to allow people to get a specific body of information in one area. The content providers in turn place buttons on their sites, enabling users to see what products YouKnowBest has and purchase them if they wish. As they purchase, YouKnowBest allows the information they gather to be saved indefinitely.

AllThingsPhoto.com, for example, is a site specializing in photographic products—single lens reflex cameras, camcorders, digital cameras, and the like, as well as accessories. It puts YouKnowBest on its site, so when a consumer downloads the application for an AllThings Photo product and buys it, YouKnowBest gets a commission—even if it's saved for a year or two and then purchased. This is the big difference between the way YouKnowBest operates and the way banner ads are used. When somebody sees a product on a banner ad, it has to be bought immediately. If there is no purchase on that click-through, the site that sent the individual there doesn't get anything. The YouKnowBest model allows them to get credit for the purchase, no matter how much later it is made.

THE TECHNOLOGY

"One big problem we had was access," says Alan Fulmer. "Most smaller vendors readily supply us with what they call data feeds, which we make available in turn to our users. Bigger companies such as Amazon.com and Wal-Mart, though, played hardball. They told us if we wanted the data we had to "crawl" their site. We had to come up with a robotlike crawler (we call it Hydra because it *is* multiheaded) that gets into those sites and extracts the data, verifying and updating it as it goes along. If you save a product for a year and then buy, Hydra will have all prices and model changes reflected as of the day you make your purchase. And the technology is so good that we can apply it in other situations as well. We have about a half-dozen patents pending."

FINDING THE NICHE

"Our competitors, we've noticed, have taken the easy route," says Alan Fulmer. "They put together a list of products, and then they act kind of like a search engine. They say to their users, 'You pick a product, and we'll go out and find all the people who sell it.' Then once you pick the product, they'll allow you to compare it.

> **OverstockedWarehouse.com**
>
> One group of sites has found a very profitable market niche based on the failure of many dot-com retailers over the past year. Patrick Byrne, chief executive of Overstock.com is aggressively buying the liquidation inventory of failed dot-coms such as the jewelry site Miadora.com, eHats.com, Baystripes.com, and ToyTime.com. According to Mr. Byrne, the average price of goods sold on Overstock was 57 percent below retail and about 20 percent below wholesale.
>
> The site relies on word-of-mouth marketing through chat rooms and e-mail, keeping advertising down. Very customer friendly, it includes shipping cost in the price, provides a liberal return policy, and responds promptly to customer inquiries.
>
> Another site with this theme is SmartBargains.com, which buys excess inventory from manufacturers and sells it at 30 to 80 percent below retail. Similarly, ReturnBuy.com accepts returned merchandise from other retailers and sells it on auction sites. Amazon.com now offers 123 categories of discount merchandise and Half.com, an eBay unit, sells used products such as books, movies, and CDs at half price or less.
>
> —Barbara Whitaker
> *The New York Times*

"So in a sense, as we go down this road trying to help people make buying decisions, we visualize our competitors as trying to hack their way through the jungle, building the road as they go. Meanwhile, we've landed by helicopter in the clearing and are using the tools we brought with us to make our way back. In other words, we've based our strategy on the technology itself, and not on the aggregation of data. Short-term focus; long-term vision."

"One of the first things we did," says Alan, "was create a dynamic spreadsheet that would be part of our application. It allows users to sort by various criteria and filter by various criteria—so that's where we wanted to start—by building the technology to create an interactive product comparison table, which allowed users to change their minds if they wanted to. And that was unique. Buying online, if you're knowledgeable, is not a scary thing. From the beginning, our intent has been to change the way people use the Internet to buy things. That broad statement has allowed us to bring people into the company with a singular goal."

But it took the YouKnowBest team a while to articulate that goal. Here are some of the ways they saw themselves over their 18-month developmental cycle:

June 1999	"KnowsBest.com, Inc. will be the first company to provide a complete independent user ratings service to all e-commerce sites."
October 1999	"We are an Internet company that knows why people buy what they buy and sells that unique buying behavior to manufacturers."
February 2000	"youknowbest.com is a free, consumer-focused convenience service that provides its members a private place to make informed and unbiased purchasing decisions."
June 2000	"youknowbest.com is a revolutionary company creating the next commerce model in the Internet world."
July 2000	"youknowbest.com is a consumer-to-business, user-controlled exchange."
September 2000	"youknowbest.com is a free, consumer-controlled shopping service that provides its members with a private place to make informed and unbiased purchasing decisions, as well as an exchange to solicit bids from merchants for their prices."
January 2001	"youknowbest.com is the first on-demand dynamic commerce content provider."

The YouKnowBest team made mistakes, but they learned from them as well. "You learn to fully embrace change," says Alan. "Actually, you go out of your way to look for change. Once you've identified your niche, you use the power of the human mind to associate seemingly dissimilar ideas and actions and coalesce them into strategies that will move your company forward."

WHAT WORKED FOR YOUKNOWBEST

Select a Problem to Solve

- All good entrepreneurial ideas (like all inventions) start with a creative way of solving a problem. There are plenty of problems with the Internet.
- Add value: When something is difficult to do, you know you are on the right track.

Apply Logic and Creativity to Solve a Problem

- People are not born visionaries, but some are better at it than others. You need to predict the future, anticipate trends, and expect the unexpected.
- Welcome "Grok"[2] change.

Listen to the World Around You to Refine Your Solution

- Every great business truly believes it is about to die.

---

[2] Grok (grohk). From the novel *Stranger in a Strange Land* by Robert Heinlein. *v.* To understand, usually in a global sense; connotes intimate and exhaustive knowledge. Source: *The Free Online Dictionary of Computing*.

- Every great business knows that what it has done can be done better.
- Stay on task. The Internet is huge and can pull you in many directions.
- Look to create a paradigm shift; differentiate yourself.
- Listen to competitors, the media, the market, customers, new employees, industry experts, and investors.
- Fear good fortune—it is one of the horsemen of the apocalypse.
- Create a culture in which everyone is free both to criticize and be criticized.
- Reward people who look for ways to do things better.

CHAPTER FIVE

The Power Brokers: Angels, Venture Capitalists, and Incubators

Paul Rand, CEO of Corporate Technology Communications, has an opinion about the naiveté of investors during the dot-com downturn beginning in 2000: "There unquestionably was a period when the people who got in early were able to capitalize, do a flip, and make a tremendous amount of money off other people's shortsightedness. It really was a game, and to think that nobody knew this was not going to come apart was just wrong. A number of smart businesspeople got into it, knowing that there was a limited potential for either revenues or earnings, but with the hope that they could make their money by investing, taking the company public, and getting their investment out—and a lot more—and then being done with it.

"And sucker be damned who ends up on the outside. The process really was a matter of letting it rise as fast and as far as it would. Then people jumped in to take advantage of it—not knowing when it was going to stop but hoping it would go on further. Eventually the natural thing just occurred, and although failures will continue in the dot-com sector, the number of start-ups based on Ponzi schemes or unsound business principles will dramatically decrease, if not go away."

DOT-COM DIARY: ANALYSIS OF A START-UP

DEVELOPING A FUNDING STRATEGY

Even so, some entrepreneurs fared better with investors during that period than others, learning as they went. Early in May of 1999, both Rob Wight and Alan Fulmer were trying to develop YouKnowBest, their dot-com start-up. But they were still full-time employees—Rob for Seagate Software, and Alan for AAA. For the most part they communicated by e-mail during the evenings, meeting once a week at the Angel, a fifties-style restaurant in Orlando, to plan and discuss their progress. During the week they exchanged ideas by e-mail. The only money going into the company was their own, and it was going into incidental expenses to keep them afloat.

In the following three memos, Rob shares with Alan his early results investigating funding to get YouKnowBest on its feet until it is able to generate revenues of its own.

> May 5, 1999
> TO: Alan
> FROM: Rob
> I just finished a conversation with a good friend and venture capitalist about initial evaluation and structure when we incorporate, which we will do when we have the site up and revenue coming in. I used the opportunity to get his opinions on number of shares, how we structure the ownership, and how much we should reserve. My goal was to get some guidance as to how his group will look at valuing us based on our business model. This is superimportant. If we get this right, I will have an easy time structuring VC deals. If we blow it, I will have a hard time.
>
> Here are some of the points to keep in mind:
>
> - Initial valuation is key. We must show improvement in stock price from the start. Share price must rise.
> - We need to have a reserve of about 15 to 20 percent of the common stock set aside for new employees/investors/partners.

- The strike price needs to be $1 or less.
- Employee performance plans are key. We need to make sure that the employees who hold significant shares of stock are still with the company when we go for funding.
- My direct involvement and ownership is going to be key when we go for funding. Essentially, the point they made was that I am the only known entity to them. That is, I have done it before. And I've worked for Microsoft. Now, if we attract someone from the high-tech space who has made money for VCs, then I will be far less important in getting funding. This means that I will need to be a full-time employee when we go for funding, or at least have a very believable vested interest in KnowsBest.com's success.

So I think we know enough now to set up the basic structure and reach agreement with others about initial shares and distribution. This should take the form of letters of understanding in the beginning and become more formalized once we incorporate.

At time of incorporation we should have:

- Initial valuation $1,000,000
- Authorized shares 1,000,000
- Price per share $1

May 6, 1999
TO: Alan
FROM: Rob
I almost forgot. They also said that they would be happy to invest $500K. I said thanks, but that we really didn't need any money right now. Maybe in a year or so—and then about $2 million.

(Says Alan: "At that point we didn't need money, but we would be looking for growth money when we were a bit further along. Four days later, Rob met with an incubator to discuss start-up strategies.")

May 11, 1999
TO: Alan
FROM: Rob

Last night I attended a venture funding meeting hosted by the Central Florida Innovation Corporation. They are a group of people acting as incubators to promote small business start-ups here in Florida.[1] They had the PriceWaterhouseCoopers venture guys there to present strategies on getting venture funding and the like.

The amount of information I got from the conference was remarkable. I could spend the next several hours typing up information. Instead, here is a summary:

- KnowsBest.com [the company's name in May 1999] needs to join CFIC. We could be one of the stars of the group.
- We need to do an angels presentation to get the local investors interested.
- There are three emerging company fund sources in Florida looking to place $100 million in the next 5 years. We need to be meeting with these people right now. This is a great adjunct to my friends the VCs. The reason we need to be talking is that we want them to check us out with my friend. This could put us in the good position of having them sell us on taking money from them.
- The average deal in Florida was midstage, for about $6 million. This is perfect for us. We don't need seed money—we want growth money.

---
[1] For a look at the way incubators work—CFIC specifically—go to www.cfic.org.

From our initial meeting with CFIC, we came up with a list of what we wanted from them:

1. Use CFIC's name to broadcast to local area investors as part of our PR
2. Help us get investors on board
3. Help create a great presentation, and a great business concept, a great business plan
4. Help figure out product pricing and product offerings; establish order of focus
5. Help create a network to attract the best employee talent
6. Supply continued support and input

SEED MONEY

Rob, Risa [Rob's wife], and Alan opted to start the company out of their own pockets. For the first 10 months of 1999 they worked out of their homes. Rob and Risa's home in Celebration, Florida, became the south campus. Alan's home, 40 miles from Rob and Risa's in Lake Mary, Florida, became the north campus.

YouKnowBest's initial employee/partners were:

Anibal Santiago—VP, Database Development
Teddy Benson—VP, Software Development
John Staubly—Creative Director
Otto Ritter—Business Development Director

The rest of the team was similarly spread north and south. All worked from their homes while working full-time jobs and met once or twice a week in the evenings and on weekends. Slowly but surely they built on and refined their idea, working simultaneously on software development, design, and a marketing plan.

> **Get Funding**
>
> - Typical investment criteria
>   - Positioned in an attractive market
>   - Strong management
>   - Proprietary technology
>   - New product development
>   - Minimum competition
>   - Follow-on products or plans
>   - Reasonable financial plan
>   - Short-term focus; long-term vision
> - Align yourself with or join a dot-com company

ROUND ONE FUNDING

"In a start-up," says Alan, "a lot of time is devoted to working on funding—at least it was in our case. We took our first serious look at funding in May 1999. A month later, we incorporated. Rob and I then created a business plan in preparation for our first pitch to investors.

"We eventually hooked up with CFIC to be our incubator. They were going to help us grow, with their main focus being to prep us for a presentation to potential investors. The deal was an initial cash payment to them and a negotiation of stock options if they were able to help us secure funding. Our team met with Richard Fox and Gordon Hogan from CFIC.

"CFIC prepared their clients for an angel investor presentation by conducting meetings with them over a 10-week period. While we found Richard and Gordon's comments on our business and business plan enlightening, we felt the process was too drawn out for an Internet company developing a competitive product on "Internet time." Our research had already shown us we couldn't wait much longer for funding. We thought that our idea was in many ways original—but not so original that a half dozen other companies couldn't come up with it given enough time, money, and insight.

"A couple of things distinguish an angel investor from a venture capital arrangement, by the way. First of all, angels work independently and spend their own money. They tend to do much smaller investments—usually from $5,000 to $500,000. Also, angels usually are not savvy about your product. (They could be relatives.) They do due diligence on potential clients, of course, but they are generalists. The group of investors we got in front of were successful businessmen who had money available for investment.

"VC companies, by contrast, tend to invest only in companies in which they have expertise. This diminishes their risk and also allows them to identify potentially synergistic alliances. Occasionally they are able to combine two client companies that may be stronger and more effective as a single entity. But usually their activities are confined to a single industry in which they feel comfortable. As to the dollar amounts, venture capital firms usually start at $1 million and go up from there. They're looking for companies that are more established to lower their risk.

"A start-up company's leverage increases with the amount of time and effort they put into it. If you go to an investor with only an "idea," you can probably expect to retain maybe 10 percent of that idea because that's all you have. Where you get to leverage your position with investors is to show them exactly what you have accomplished during the year or however long you've been working on the idea. The more results you can demonstrate, the larger your sweat equity reward.

"As it turned out, our conversations with Rob's venture capital friends were moving forward at the same time as our meetings with CFIC. In the end we were able to make a pitch to Aweida Venture Management. It worked! They liked our plan well enough to commit to approximately $1 million of funding.

"About a week later we finished our course with CFIC and made our presentation to their angel investors, as we were obligated to do. This presentation was most enjoyable for us. At the end of that meeting we let them know that we had secured first-round funding and were not looking for additional investment until perhaps the next round. Whether it was our presentation or our telling them that we didn't need their money (probably a combination of both), we were surrounded by several of these investors who wanted to invest right then. We took names and promised we would contact them. On our way out, we couldn't resist smiling at each other at the irony of being offered all this money that we now didn't need.

Seeking Capital, They Found Jobs Instead

In 1999, Brian Flynn and Vince Trantolo left the corporate world to solicit funding for an idea delivering both content and commerce to handheld devices.

"Vince and I had talked for years about doing something on our own," says Brian, "and all of a sudden the talk became real."

"I put together a business plan," says Vince, "and together we built a business model, the marketing, and everything else that would have to go into it. Now all we needed was the seed funding."

The two entrepreneurs made a number of presentations without success. Then Brian's wife, a trade publishing editor, suggested they talk with Dr. Edwin Schlossberger, author of a book she had edited and a successful owner of several interactive media and entertainment companies, all of which he had founded himself. Brian and Vince read Ed's books, called for an appointment, and went in to execute their well-practiced pitch.

"About three-quarters of the way through our meeting," says Brian, "we realized that we weren't pitching him; he was interviewing us.

"We left and met with Ed again in about 3 weeks. He said, 'Okay, are you interested?' We said, 'Interested in what?' It turned out he had done some research on us and thought we would be a

continued on next page

> good team to put together another company he had been contemplating. He had us meet with people in his company to get validation from both sides."
>
> "So we went away and thought about it," says Vince. "We finally realized that it was a good situation for us, to step in and really build something. We would have access to Ed's connections and also be able to bring in some of our own contacts. It seemed like a really good fit, and it was a full-blown idea as opposed to our haphazardly trying to start something from nothing. The offices were there; the funding was there; and there was enough structure to get us up and running."
>
> "Right," says Brian. "We had a prototype and an idea of how the model might work. We took it from there to an analysis of the real business model and the customers. We worked out the technology solution, built the management team, and now we're looking for additional partnerships that can take us to the next level."
>
> To see what Brian (chief executive officer) and Vince (chief operating officer) have created—backed by Dr. Schlossberger's resources and vision—go to http://www.annotate.net.

ROUND-TWO FUNDING

"With the boost from Aweida Venture Management," continues Alan, "we all made the leap in mid-October 1999. Actually, Rob had quit Seagate Software in June. The rest of us who were working full-time jobs also quit. Rob and I set up an office in the apartment over his garage in Celebration, Florida. We spent our first 2 weeks looking for office space and equipment in anticipation of the others coming on board. We bought a few computers and other equipment, put up temporary walls and bookcases, and built rudimentary furniture so the rest of the team wouldn't have to work on the floor when they came in a week later. One of the advantages of working out of Celebration—which is owned by Disney—

is that the entire community is pre-wired. All we did was plug our computers and other equipment right into the wall, and we were hooked up to the Internet from Day One.

"From November 1999 until the following March, we were in a 4000-square-foot office, which at that time we enlarged to 7000 square feet. We stayed there until about September, at which time we had 20 employees. Now we're up to 43 employees, and we've moved into another building in Celebration that just went up. Our space here is about 20,000 square feet.

"Our goals for the second-round funding were to find either another well-established venture capital firm to join Aweida Venture Management or to find an investor in Florida. Through relationships Aweida management had in the VC community, we were able to schedule meetings with two large venture capital firms in the San Francisco Bay Area. Rob Wight, Teddy Benson, and I made the trip in February 2000. What we noticed during this trip was that advertising for dot-com companies dominated billboards, the sides of buses, the tops of cabs. There was no mistaking that we were in the middle of a start-up bonanza. 'You are not alone,' echoed in our ears. We became even more anxious to get our site up and running.

"At our first meeting we could barely see the receptionist for the 3-foot stack of FedEx packages on her desk. She said these were all business plans that had arrived that day! We spent about 2 hours showing this group our PowerPoint presentation and a demo, and answering their questions.

"Our second meeting was with the senior partner of another large VC firm, took about the same length of time, and met with the same result. What became obvious was that we were too early in our development cycle to make a positive impression on these venture capitalists. We needed more product, and we needed to demonstrate more effectively that we could separate ourselves from our competitors.

"Two months later the market took a nosedive. Investors got scared and started to pull out of start-up dot-coms. Our competitors started closing shop because they didn't have sustainable business plans. Actually, this was a good time for us. We had been conservative in the way we raised money and conservative in the way we spent it. Watching other companies fold motivated us. It also made it easier for us to develop our technology.

"Meanwhile, we met with a newly formed VC group from Sarasota, Florida, called New South Ventures. They had seen us at another presentation and were interested in investing in us. So we closed our second round of funding with an investment from New South Ventures and an additional investment from Aweida.

"On March 16, 2001, we became operational. In the first 2 weeks, 1100 consumers downloaded our software and used our program. It was an exciting time. At that point we moved out of the development phase and into a customer-focused phase. The plan now is simple. Work toward profitability."

THE FUTURE

"We have worked with an incubator, a venture capital company, and an angel investor. We need no more outside money. Every employee of the company holds stock options. Our job now is to ensure that our shareholders get a generous return on their investment.

"Our hope is that several people in YouKnowBest will become wildly successful and rich as they contribute to the company's success. We know too that some of them will leave to pursue their own ideas. From the beginning we hoped to build a network of entrepreneurs and investors that can continue to grow great companies here in central Florida. That is our dream.

"Last week a student at a university at which we gave one of our entrepreneurial presentations asked me to be his mentor. This is one of the fringe benefits that makes building such an enterprise worthwhile."

WHAT WORKED FOR YOUKNOWBEST

Know What All Investors Want and Create a Business Plan That Shows It

- Be in an attractive market.
- Attract strong management.
- Build proprietary technology.
- Utilize innovative product development.
- Stress minimum competition.
- Create follow-on products or plans.
- Put together a reasonable financial plan.
- Emphasize short-term focus and long-term vision.

Build Value First

- Start with an idea that will assure the VC 10 times its investment.
- If it were easy, it already would have been done.
- Quick is not as important as valuable.
- Embrace "no." Look for things that are hard. When things get easy, make them hard again.
- Don't take the easy road, no matter how much you want to.
- Change is your friend.

Refine Your Elevator Speech

- Incubators, angel investors, and venture capitalists are all interested in your elevator speech—the 30-second speech that embodies your company's mission, differentiation, and benefits.

Make Your Investors Your Friends

- Find great investors.
- Develop a trusting relationship: be trustworthy; avoid surprises; think conservative.
- Make your investor your partner; valuation means nothing to an unfunded business.
- Listen to your investors; use board meetings to learn.
- Work hard.

CHAPTER SIX

Building a Killer Management Team

The best mission, the most copious funding, the most ideally positioned market niche—all are worthless if the right people are not hired to build the machine and make it go.

"Entrepreneurs sometimes find that hiring people with diverse skills does not come naturally," says Desh Deshpande, chairman of Sycamore Networks. "Good engineers will want to hire good engineers, for instance, but not necessarily a strong finance or sales person. But the founder must hire people who complement his or her strengths. So one way to begin the hiring process is to identify your own strengths and weaknesses. This will tell you whom you need to hire first. When you and a few people form the core of the company, you will look for people who are strong where you and the team may be weak."

STAFFING GROWING PAINS

In the spring of 1999, YouKnowBest was just beginning to define itself as a company. "Early on, we made some staffing mistakes," says Alan

> ## Don't Let Success Go to Your Head
>
> What's one tough lesson that I've learned about doing business on the Internet? It's important to have a diverse team. I'm not talking about just gender or race. I mean diversity of skills and temperament. It's hard to get your team composition right.
>
> At the beginning, you need more diversity than you can imagine. When we started iVillage, we didn't have enough technical people or really anal analytical people. Instead, we had a surplus of people who could sell our story to customers and advertisers—which is great. But you still need people to build the subways. That lack of diversity slowed us down in the beginning.
>
> But as critical as diversity is at the beginning, once you start to scale, you want the opposite—a team of minds that think alike. Otherwise, you get gridlock. As iVillage grew, creative gridlock threatened our team's cohesiveness. I had to deal with intuitive people, analytical people, lyrical people, and worrywarts. It took a lot of work to get everyone to trust one another.
>
> An added challenge, of course, was managing people during the overhyped, dysfunctional universe of the Internet boom. In the end, you're crazy to let any kind of success go to your head. The moment when everything seems to be going your way is exactly when you should be looking over your shoulder and asking, "What's brewing?"
>
> —Candice Carpenter, Chairman, iVillage
> *Fast Company*
> February 2001

Fulmer. "We found a product development team we thought would work out, but they were not completely comfortable with what we were doing. At that point we were not funded and were all working on spec. The only money that had been put into the company at all was our own money—and it wasn't paying any salaries. Anyone who joined us at that point was going to be working on spec. We were all working out of our own homes. The development team we hired wasn't at all comfortable in

> **Find the Right People**
>
> - Work your network of friends.
> - Advertise.
> - Work the network of friends of new hires.
> - Get professional assistance.
>
> —YouKnowBest presentation

this situation. They stayed with us for a month or so and then just got cold feet and backed out. It became obvious that we needed to develop a system that would get us the best people and was not determined by a hit-or-miss methodology."

THE GAUNTLET

Over the next several months, different members of the team provided input into a more formal hiring strategy. Eventually a codified system emerged that with minor adjustments is still in place today. The key element is a half-day interview called the gauntlet. "We tell people that the process involves anywhere from four to eight interviews," says Alan Fulmer.

"We say this not because the availability of interviewers varies from day to day. The interview track is always preset, with seven interviewers, at a minimum, always available on the designated day. The reason is that by giving a four-to-eight-interview range we can cut short the track without the risk of humiliating the candidate."

There are strict guidelines in setting up the gauntlet. The first two interviews are almost always people from the same department as the person being interviewed. In other words, if the interviewee is a software developer, then the first two interviewers will be software developers. The last person in the interview track is always the decision maker. Everyone else is there just to evaluate and recommend. While Rob and

Alan are not usually the final decision makers, one or both of them are part of the interview track for just about every employment interview that has been conducted.

Interviewers are not restricted to senior staff. Most interviews are likely to include the potential direct supervisor of the individual being interviewed, peers of the person being interviewed, and people who would work for the interviewee. Says Alan: "People I've talked with outside the company find it hard to believe that a subordinate to a potential employee could be part of the hiring process. But think about it. Wouldn't you like to be able to interview the person who is coming in to be your boss? This actually can help ensure that the entire department is going to work well together."

Alan believes that the toughest part of the gauntlet is interviewing with Rob, who has the ability to create questions where there appear to be two equally valid, and perhaps equally wrong, answers. "The objective is to put the candidate in a predicament and see what he or she does. We want to see if candidates can generate ideas, work through problems, and build arguments in support of their rationale for any given decision. We have had interview sessions cut off in midprocess when the candidates were incapable of generating any ideas to solve a problem or if their only response was to attempt to do or say what they thought the interviewer wanted."

The Spiral Staircase

- Get a great idea.
- Find the right people.
- Put support services in place.
- Get funding.
- Put infrastructure in place.
- Get a great idea.

—YouKnowBest presentation

As soon as YouKnowBest interviewers complete a session in the interview track, they are required to immediately send an e-mail to everyone else on the track. The e-mail includes four things:

- A hire/no hire recommendation
- A recommendation as to the interviewee's level in the company
- The interviewee's job title
- Pros and cons regarding the interviewee's candidacy

If an interviewer is unable to complete a line of questioning, or if the interview leads to other unresolved questions, this is added to the e-mail for follow-up.

Four "no hire" recommendations result in a termination of the interview. Termination can be as abrupt as the decision maker saying, "Sorry. This doesn't seem to be working out," or a more congenial, "Do you have any questions?" exit. Of the 50 or so people who have been offered positions, only one or two have ever gone through the gauntlet without getting at least one "no hire."

One or more people in the interview track will tell the interviewee about the company, the culture, and the mission. The interviewee is always allowed the opportunity to ask questions because these can be a useful gauge to the interviewer in determining preparation, intelligence, and a desire to learn.

"We are looking for people who are interested in a career, not just a job," says Alan. "Every person who is hired becomes a shareholder in the company. So it is the responsibility of the people in the interview track to understand that they are recommending that this person become an owner/shareholder. One of the questions that floats in the back of everyone's head is, 'If I had to leave the company, would I entrust the company to this person?'"

"We have had people cry in the middle of this process. Some have gotten partway through and decided on their own that they are not right for the job and stopped the interview."

> **Performance of Shareholders**
>
> - Actively participate in all discussions.
> - Look for opportunities to improve our site and our business.
> - Scour the Web for information on products, competitors, possible acquisitions, content sources, technology we can use, or industry trends—make yourself an expert on what we are doing.
> - Ask questions—continually learn and expand your own intellectual base.
> - Provide a leadership role.
> - Help those around you accomplish their tasks—not by doing their work for them, but by supporting them.
> - Anticipate areas in which the company may have problems and be prepared to solve them.
> - Show your dedication and commitment to the company in whatever way possible.
> - Do your job well.
> - Make good decisions.
> - Be constructive.
> - Exceed expectations.
>
> —YouKnowBest presentation

"What we have found is that people with experience as contractors have a hard time making the transition to becoming a shareholder of a start-up. Contracting is a very individual, independent way of life. Being part of a start-up is just the opposite. It is all about working as a team, being flexible, and working long hours without additional pay. Some can make this transition. Many cannot. Out of 3000 résumés, about 6 percent have made it to the interview stage. About one in two make it through the first interview. Those who make it all the way through the interview have a 50:50 chance of being offered a position.

"Why do we put so much effort into hiring? It comes down to the fact that smart people don't work for mediocre people. You have to be tough.

You have to ask the right questions. The people you hire have to fit in the company, understand the culture, and fulfill the needs of the position. It is well worth a half-day of interviewing to ensure that we get it right.

"Do we always get it right? No. In our first year we hired some people who didn't work out. We probably had an attrition rate of about 10 percent. But we've gotten much better. In our second year the attrition rate has dropped to 0 percent."

WHAT WORKED FOR YOUKNOWBEST

Identify Areas in Which You Need Expertise

- Once you have your direction as a business, determine the talent that will be needed to get you there.
- Don't acquire more or less staff than you need.
- Be open to hiring the person you didn't know you needed.

Hire Smart People

- Smart people don't hire mediocre people. As soon as you hire a mediocre person, you compromise the future of your company.
- Look for energy, passion, assertiveness, success, failure, industry knowledge, experience working in complex situations, strong work ethic, trustworthiness, intelligence, and high tolerance for risk.
- Allow employees to grow (smart trumps job title).
- Everyone evaluates everyone.

Give Incentives

- Zero politics—everyone gets an office; every office and desk is the same size.

- Anyone who knows a candidate cannot be involved in that hire.
- Job levels matter more than organizational structure.
- Everyone is a shareholder.
- All meetings are open—no secrets; there is always freedom to comment.
- Challenge everyone to change the world.

PART THREE

Identifying the Match: What It Takes to Fit In

"What kind of match am I trying to fit into?" might be the first question to ask yourself. When you get that answer, find out if you fit in—or are likely to. Now you're ready for the "where" question. You'll be pleased to know this question is multiple choice.

CHAPTER SEVEN

Culture Shock Beyond Dress Code

It's all true. Regardless of your specialty, there are many differences between traditional companies and an Internet company—some apparent and some real. There are also a number of differences that distinguish one Web company from another, characterized in part by whether the company is a start-up or a more established firm, and in part by internal philosophy. In the volatile surreality of dot-com start-ups in particular, business models change from week to week. Funding is awarded one day, only to be withdrawn the next. In such situations the best skill set may also call for steel nerves and infinite optimism. But don't despair—more of these companies make it than not, irrespective of the horror stories chronicled in Chapter 1.

But there is also room for mistakes. A number of dot-com employees have found the atmosphere anathema for any one of a number of reasons and have returned to the world of brick and mortar—or even of clicks and mortar. This is particularly true of those career changers drawn to dot-com start-ups, only to realize that they are unable or unwilling to make the sacrifices required of them.

IDENTIFYING THE MATCH: WHAT IT TAKES TO FIT IN

Inside View

Paul Andriotti—Start-Up Victim . . . and Survivor

In 1998, quality assurance specialist Paul Andriotti (not his real name) joined a small dot-com wireless company that had successfully gone through its second round of funding. Things looked great for the first few months but fell apart quickly to become a complete nightmare. Here Paul recalls some of the particulars.

Q How did it all begin?
A First of all, I graduated from Waitfield State College in 1992 with a communications degree. At the time the job market was pretty rotten for recent college grads, so I took a few courses in computer-aided drafting at a local community college.

Q Why those particular courses?
A One of my friends was an engineer making money doing drafting on the side. It looked kind of interesting, and I thought I could get a job doing it, which turned out to be the case. I worked for them for 4 years, and it was actually pretty boring. I went back to UMass and started taking some night courses in Unix and programming, and started looking for jobs. Finally after 20 interviews or so I got a job as an intern doing desktop support.

   This company was trying to produce a client/server type of software to speed up Internet connections. They really couldn't make a go of that so they switched to hardware, which made a lot of us nervous. Everybody thought they were going to fold, so my boss convinced me and a couple of others to go with him to a start-up. He said it was going to be a real successful company, and it was a shorter commute, so I decided to try it.

Q What was your specific job?
A When I switched jobs I was supposed to be a network administrator, but it didn't work out that way. I complained, but nobody paid atten-

continued on next page

tion. Then toward the end of the summer we started hearing rumblings. Major rumors got out that we were definitely closing, and morale dropped like a stone. Those last 2 months people would bring their own martini glasses, and we had a couple of refrigerators that were always stocked with beer. I'd try to be there a solid 10 hours, and occasionally I stayed overnight, as we were expected to because there were a lot of loose ends to keep track of. But even then half the people would be drunk and useless, and I'm thinking "Why am I here?" One night I fell asleep in the QA [quality assurance] lab on a futon.

Management wasn't making their schedules. (And these were the same guys who convinced the venture capitalists that they were God's gift to dot-com. My boss, age 28, was making six figures. Another woman I worked with—also age 28—was making six figures.) It was a circus—people would go behind the building and smoke marijuana. It's no wonder the place went out of business. The irony is that a big reason I went there was to learn proper QA procedures. What a joke.

Q So what finally happened?
A When it all fell apart, I decided I really wanted to be someplace more established. I'm at a security company now that has been around for 15 years. I'm doing software quality assurance, a job I like. Actually, being in the dot-com wasn't all bad. There's a certain camaraderie, everybody is young, and you meet some great people. If you don't mind putting up with the insanity, you can learn a lot and sharpen your technical skills.

Hundreds of others are lured from existing jobs with the promise of big paychecks and stock options, only to learn too late that the job was not what it appeared to be. For one reason or another the fit was all wrong—though this could have been determined with more rigorous investigation before the interview(s), and more rigorous questioning *during* the interview(s). See Chapter 11 to avoid these mistakes yourself.

IDENTIFYING THE MATCH: WHAT IT TAKES TO FIT IN

THE RIGHT STUFF

But let's start with what it takes to qualify for a position with an Internet company. One way to find out is to page through the job descriptions in Chapter 8, and see which of them matches your interests, education, and skill sets. As you'll see, with the proliferation of job opportunities in new media and desktop publishing companies, this does not necessarily require a computer science degree. Those of you who are in the first year or two of college still have time to adjust your curriculum to meet minimum academic requirements for your specialty. Below, as an example, are the core courses in Boston College's Carroll School of Management, followed by required courses for two subspecialty majors:

    Introduction to Ethics
    Principles of Economics (Micro)
    Principles of Economics (Macro)
    Computers for Management
    Financial Accounting
    Managerial Accounting
    Statistics
    Introduction to Law
    Organizational Behavior
    Management and Operations
    Basic Finance
    Basic Marketing
    Strategy and Policy
    Foreign language requirement

COMPUTER SCIENCE MAJOR
    Computer Science I
    Computer Science II
    Computer Organization and Assembly Language
    (Two additional computer science courses)

INFORMATION SYSTEMS MAJOR
   Computer Science I
   Systems Analysis
   Business Systems
   (One additional computer science course, or one electronic commerce or management information systems course, both under the Management and Operations department)

INTERNSHIPS

No better way exists for a college student to get a feel for employment in the real world than to simulate the experience as an intern—either paid or unpaid. A lot can be learned on several levels over a summer or even during the school year if schedules can be worked out. If you are uncertain about the industry or function you have selected, an internship can give you a warts-and-all insider's view that could save you several years in the wrong place—or it could reinforce a first impression that told you this was where you belonged all along.

The search engine Google lists about 500,000 internship-related entries. Rising Star Internships (www.rsinternships.com), as an example, maintains a Web site for students, employers, and schools, and includes 12 computer- and Internet/new media categories. WetFeet.com (see Chapter 1) manages an internship program involving some 200,000 students, several thousand college career centers, and 3,000 companies nationwide—from nonprofits to *Fortune* 500s.

"From the beginning, our mission has been to educate job candidates about what it's *really* like to work for different companies and in different industries," says WetFeet CEO Gary Alpert. "As we built our business, we learned that internships were becoming a more important part of the overall recruiting strategy. From the corporate perspective, internship programs are thought of as being an investment in recruiting top talent down the road, as well as preparing them to make an immediate contribution to whatever company they join.

IDENTIFYING THE MATCH: WHAT IT TAKES TO FIT IN

"From the perspective of the schools and their career centers, it is very much in their interest to promote the services we offer because we are helping both sides and there is no cost to the school. Our program is the largest and most up-to-date of its kind on the Web."

Student alert: Start first with your own career center to see what internship programs are active nearby in your specialty. Many companies offer not only a salary/stipend arrangement but college credit as well.

ARE YOU INTERNET MATERIAL?

The demand for experienced executives who can provide cyberspace corporate leadership is far greater than the supply. Not everyone—no matter how accomplished or dedicated—has the ability to succeed in the alien upstart Internet world. And among those more than moderately interested in getting a handle on such a topic are the executive recruiters.

One firm, Russell Reynolds Associates, was able to develop a diagnostic tool based on interviews with leading Internet executives regarding their approach to making decisions, meeting challenges, and executing ideas. They analyzed common themes, skills, and approaches to arrive at a set of characteristics they call *Web DNA*, identifying individuals who reach the highest levels of success in the online environment. According to the results of this survey, owners of Web DNA exhibit the following six qualities:

1. *They recognize opportunity.* Executives with Web DNA seize the day and jump on fresh business concepts, new business models, and innovative operating tools—and otherwise further their business with a minimum of delay.
2. *They radiate vision.* Evangelical in projecting their beliefs about their business, these executives stay focused and make it their priority to communicate their vision persistently to the entire organization.

3. *They have an 80/20 mindset.* They know that it's better to be 80 percent right today than 100 percent right tomorrow. Faced with incomplete information, they have the experience and insight to fill in the blanks.
4. *They get the "right stuff" done.* Seeking value from all activity, they keep themselves from getting distracted into tangential tasks with little payoff.
5. *They are organizational improvisers.* Developing variations of standard business and organizational models, these leaders build and maintain fluid organizations responsive to customer needs and competitor moves. The right people are in the right place to respond swiftly and effectively.
6. *They are learning-obsessed.* Constantly in the feedback loop and incorporating significant new information, successful Internet executives continually seek data to assess business models, evaluate trends, and learn—and they hold themselves to high personal standards of continual self-examination and self-improvement.

If more than half of these characteristics describes you, likely as not you could be happy and successful in the dot-com world. The operative word in that sentence, of course, is "could." There are a number of considerations to keep in mind before committing to life on the "other side." Some of them are dealt with on the remaining pages of this chapter. (To take the Web DNA quiz and receive an analysis of your quiz score, go to www.russellreynolds.com/industry/internet/webDNA.asp.)

Becky Stein, a Russell Reynolds recruiter who specializes in Internet search assignments, says the first question people thinking about an Internet position should ask themselves is "Why do I really want to do this?"

"Half of the people moving to the Internet economy are doing it for the wrong reasons," says Stein. "We're not interested in people who want to make a quick buck. We're looking for people who are in it for the long haul, who see the Internet as a better way of doing business. I've got to be careful about the motivation issue when I meet candidates."

Wanted: Volunteers for the Techie Peace Corps

After founding and successfully building Tripod, Inc., a Web-hosting site, Ethan Zuckerman took some time off to decide what to do next. He recalled a year he spent in Ghana as a Fulbright visiting scholar. It was a powerful experience. "I discovered firsthand the meaning of poverty," he says.

Then he had it: a way to bring technical know-how to needy countries. He set up a nonprofit organization from his base in North Adams, Massachusetts—Geekcorps (www.geekcorps.org)—put in some of his own money, and hired a staff. He then returned to Ghana to find out how the GeekCorps could do the most good. By September 2000, six volunteers were on their way to Ghana.

Each volunteer was matched with a company that had a specific need. Volunteers worked for free. In exchange, the company would put money into a community project. Says Zuckerman: "I looked for people who understood the new economy, who had worked for a dot-com, had prior volunteer experience, and were psyched about community service. They also had to be flexible and have a sense of humor."

The first group spent 3 months in Ghana, just long enough to get acclimated to the culture and do some real good. Surprisingly, most companies where volunteers had jobs were willing to grant them sabbaticals. They figured the experience would make them even more valuable employees.

Zuckerman's goal is to have 500 volunteers working in 15 countries within 5 years. He envisions the GeekCorps as a potential matchmaker for funding foreign businesses with venture capital funding.

—Bob Weinstein
Adapted from the *Chicago Sun-Times*

WHAT IS IT LIKE TO WORK IN AN INTERNET COMPANY?

The obvious pluses and minuses of working in a dot-com company have made their way into job search and career change lore. Some of these generalizations are accurate, some hold up for the most part but may no longer be true, and some are either flat-out aberrations or exaggerations.

Dot-Com Feng Shui

Some dot-com start-ups are becoming change agents in the character of the workplace itself. They join a number of enlightened brick-and-mortar companies that have embraced a revolutionary approach to office environment. In some instances this was inadvertent—caused more by the exigencies of starting a business from scratch than from any innovative spirit. In the formative months before funding kicks in, conventional perks such as plush offices and teak furniture for top management must wait. Instead, bosses and grunts alike often find themselves lodged in the same open area. With a blurred hierarchy, the emphasis is on cross-training—sometimes across functional lines—rather than on dotted-line reporting schemes. This can easily lead to a frontier, we're-all-in-it-together mentality, dictated nonetheless by practical considerations.

But some new-economy companies that embraced austere beginnings out of necessity have learned that their Spartan physical settings can lead to lasting positive, synergistic results.

"The parallels between neighborhoods and offices are striking," writes Malcolm Gladwell in *The New Yorker*. The old order of high-ranking employees inside lush offices guarded by secretaries Gladwell calls suburbs. Replacing this system in many technology companies are "busy public spaces, open-plan areas without walls, executives next to the newest hires," the office equivalent of houses and shops mixed together. "The hush of the traditional office," says Gladwell, "has been supplanted by something much closer to the noisy, bustling ballet of [Greenwich Village]."

IDENTIFYING THE MATCH: WHAT IT TAKES TO FIT IN

When George Colony, CEO of Forrester Research, suggested in 1994 forming a "pod" of 8 to 10 core people to work together in one large room, "Everyone screamed," he remembers. "They would only agree to the idea if I joined them, and nobody believed I would. But one day I came in, put all of my stuff in boxes, and moved into the pod. That's how it began. That new team lit the company on fire. We shared our tears and our fears, and at the end of the year we danced on our desks to celebrate our success."

Many successful Internet companies are able to project the laid-back atmosphere and informal setting of a dot-com start-up and the stability of a third-generation *Fortune* 500 multinational. One of these is Google, based in Mountain View, California, currently the world's largest search engine. Here is its enviable catalog of perks and benefits:

- Health care:
  Medical insurance (options from four carriers)
  Vision insurance (one exam and lenses per year)
  Dental insurance (comprehensive, plus 100 percent preventive coverage)

How Dot-Coms Are Reshaping the Workplace

New kinds of companies and new technologies like the Net are reinventing the way many of us work, according to a study by CDI@Work and MIT's Sloan School of Management. The number of positions filled by temporary staffing companies grew to 3.23 million from 1.35 million between 1988 and 1998, the fastest employment growth of any industry sector. Today, more than 25 percent of American workers are part-timers, independent contractors, or temps, the study found. When contract and on-call work is included, the share of the nation's workforce operating outside traditional, full-time jobs has mushroomed to nearly 30 percent.

—Jon Katz
Yahoo! Internet Life

- Stocks: As stated in formal offer letter; vest over 4-year period
- Vacation:
  Year 1: 15 days
  Year 3: 20 days
  Year 5: 25 days
- Holidays: Nine paid; sick days as necessary
- Pretax Savings: 401(k) plan (employee contributes, Google matches, to $2200/yr)
  Ten available investment options
- Protection:
  Group life insurance (two times annual salary)
  Short-term disability (60 percent of salary, 30 days from last worked)
  Long-term disability ($66\frac{2}{3}$ percent of salary, after 90 days)
- Referral:
  Employee assistance (confidential counseling, including dependents)
  Legal counsel for common legal issues
- Gourmet lunch (free lunch 5 days/week, plus breakfast food and free snacks)
- Massage and gym (massage therapists, gym, and sauna all available on-site)
- Activities:
  Weekly hockey games; bike rides; walks in wildlife preserve
  Grand piano in lobby open to all

Don't count on such an across-the-board availability of such benefits packages during your search for the ideal company. (Getting as close to it as you can, however, is an objective worth pursuing.) Actually, beginning in early 2001, a backlash against the more egregious 24/7 boomtime excesses was well underway. The premature death of so many dot-coms, as well as a general slowing of the economy, sharply diminished the allocation of free Porsches and fancy parties. Cost-consciousness was in; sleeping

> ## Au Revoir, Geek Chic
>
> As dot-coms go down in flames, there's a growing concern among employers that dress-down days have gone too far. Cleveland-based Management Recruiters International found 34 percent of 3000 employers surveyed report that many employees' idea of business-casual dress is too casual for the office.
>
> Joseph Abboud, president of the New York menswear firm that bears his name, said the casual dress trend was part of the Silicon Valley attitude that you can wear whatever you want and still become a millionaire. "A lot of new-generation workers are finding that they are going to have to prove themselves at more traditional firms, and that includes dressing differently," he said.
>
> His younger clients are moving away from jeans to sport coats, dress slacks, and suits, Abboud said—no doubt with a sigh of relief.
>
> —T. Shawn Taylor
> The *Chicago Tribune*

bags in the office were out—which is to say that a normalization of the workday may be coming to the dot-coms.

Due Diligence

What makes a good company a good company? What should a prospective employee look for in trying to decide whether a match is a good one? Paul Rand gave considerable thought to this question when he was putting together his Chicago-based public relations firm, Corporate Technology Communications (www.ctcomm.com), which after only 3 years is the largest B2B technology-focused PR firm in the Midwest—and a leader nationally.

"We had to find out in a hurry how to attract people into a company with an unproven track record," says Rand, "and ask them to leave a more established opportunity to do so. We're in a service business, and people are our principal asset. Clients go with an organization because they like, respect, and trust the people—as well as what the organization stands for. So the only way to assure consistency in the people we hired was to formally articulate what was important to us and be sure these principles were reflected in the people who represented us on a day-to-day basis."

Rand and his management team came up with a list of "basic yet essential principles" intended to tell prospective employees and clients alike what they could expect by forming a bond with Corporate Technology Communications, all under the heading "We practice the following":

- We trust one another.
- We speak the truth.
- We both lead and follow.
- We take responsibility.
- We have the right to say "no."
- We make a difference.
- We have unique lives.
- We strive for consistency.
- We think of risks as opportunities.
- We believe that fun is both a tool and an outcome.

"We wanted to set up a self-screener for companies that were looking for partners with the kinds of values we shared, and for individuals who would do the best job without having to work 24 hours a day," says Rand. "So if you can put a line in the sand that makes you more specific about the kinds of people who will be successful in your organization, you will also find the kinds of clients with which you will be successful. It helps assure that everybody wins all around."

Do enough of your own due diligence to be sure your target companies pass muster for whatever criteria are essential to you. (Some investigative techniques can be found in Chapter 10; some useful interview strategies appear in Chapter 11. Company documents you should examine include

> ### Uh-Oh, Due Diligence Alert
>
> A global study released by Kroll Associates reports that Internet executives are four times more likely to have "unsavory backgrounds" than executives from other industries. Of the 70 background investigations of Internet executives and board members conducted by Kroll, 39 percent were found to have problems relating to insurance fraud, undisclosed bankruptcies, securities violations, and even links to organized crime. "The whole effort has been to move at Internet speed, which has meant not stopping to do careful checks on employees or putting in place internal auditing or security," said Ernie Brod, executive managing director of Kroll's New York office.
>
> —*Financial Times*
> October 24, 2000

the business plan, table of organization, annual report, biographies of all officers and board of directors, and relevant press releases. Also talk to competitors, customers, vendors, and industry analysts. If you're working with a recruiter, ask him or her to assist in your research. Finally, find out who the company's backers are and what their track record is. It's impossible to have too much information for a decision as important as this.

CHAPTER EIGHT

What Kind of Job Are You Looking For?

The U.S. Bureau of Labor Statistics projects a brighter future for computer-related companies than for those in any other industry, until at least the year 2008. Four occupations alone will add more than 1.5 million jobs:

Computer systems analysts	577,000 new jobs
Computer support specialists	439,000 new jobs
Computer engineers	323,000 new jobs
Computer programmers	198,000 new jobs

These figures represent nearly a 100 percent increase from the number of jobs that existed in these same specialties in 1998. Total employment is expected to increase by an estimated 20 million jobs in dozens of occupations between 1998 and 2008. These include many of the positions that exist as well in conventional companies, among them in the functions of human resources, corporate communications, marketing, and sales.

IDENTIFYING THE MATCH: WHAT IT TAKES TO FIT IN

COMPUTER-RELATED CAREERS

The Internet and computer-related job titles described on the following pages are broken down into four categories: hardware, software, new media, and support. These don't cover all the possibilities, to be sure. At the end of this chapter are several sources that will lead you to more information about your specialty. Salary levels for each of these occupations vary widely in different parts of the country. See Chapter 12 to learn what various jobs pay in metropolitan areas of interest to you. Web sites for the professional organizations listed after most occupations usually include certification information as well as employment sources and opportunities.

Hardware

Computer hardware systems include the computers themselves, computer components, peripherals (such as joysticks, modems, and printers), chips, boards, circuitry, and other electronic equipment.

COMPUTER ENGINEERS
What they do. Computer engineers design, build, test, and evaluate computer systems, peripheral devices, circuit boards, and computer chips. They work with both the hardware and software aspects of systems design and development. They usually apply the theories and principles of science and mathematics to design hardware, software, networks, and processes and to solve technical problems. Even though their work emphasizes the application of theory, computer engineers are also involved in building prototypes. They often work as part of a team that designs new computing devices or computer-related equipment, systems, or software. Likely employers are hardware manufacturers, and engineering and design firms.

- *Hardware engineers* usually design, develop, test, and supervise the manufacture of computer hardware such as chips or device controllers.

- *Development engineers* often work in research and development (R&D) departments of computer firms that originate new product ideas.
- *Production engineers* supervise the production process in manufacturing the product once it has been designed. Production engineers require management as well as engineering skills.
- *Quality assurance engineers* control the production process, making sure that the product is manufactured properly and that no flaws occur in production.

Engineers often use computer-aided design (CAD) to produce and analyze designs. Computer-aided design is made possible by powerful design software, automating the drafting and design process for mechanical and electronic applications. With CAD, engineers can create three-dimensional models of objects that can be manipulated by computer. As a result, engineers can experiment with different designs that would be too costly to produce manually.

Computer engineers also have to know programming. While FORTRAN used to be the programming language of choice, C has supplanted FORTRAN in the microcomputer field. In addition to mainframe, midsize, and microcomputer design, some computer engineers design industrial robots, automated systems, and artificial intelligence–based hardware systems.

Getting in and moving up. Computer hardware engineers usually need a bachelor's degree in computer engineering or electrical engineering. A Ph.D. in computer science or engineering—or at least a master's degree—is usually required for jobs in research labs or universities. Employers usually look for people who have broad knowledge and experience in computer systems and technologies, strong problem solving and analytical skills, and good interpersonal skills. Courses in computer programming or systems design are good preparation for a job in this field.

Computer engineers employed in industry may advance into managerial or project leadership positions. Those in colleges and universities can become heads of research departments or published authorities in their specialty.

Employment forecast and earnings. Computer engineers and scientists are expected to be among the fastest growing occupations through 2008. Growth will be driven by a highly increasing demand for computer and data processing services, which is projected to be the fastest-growing industry in the U.S. economy.

Median annual earnings of computer engineers were nearly $62,000 in 1998. The lowest 10 percent earned about $37,000, and the highest 10 percent earned almost $93,000.

Professional connections. The following Web sites provide information about organizations that may be helpful to your job search.

Association for Computing Machinery (ACM), 1515 Broadway, New York, NY 10036   http://www.acm.org

Quality Assurance Institute, 7575 Fr. Phillips Blvd., Suite 350, Orlando, FL 32819   http://www.qai.org

SYSTEMS ANALYSTS

What they do. Systems analysts solve computer problems and enable computer technology to meet the needs of an organization. They plan and develop new computer systems or devise ways to apply existing systems' resources to additional operations. They may also design new systems, including both hardware and software, or add a new software application to capitalize on the computer's power.

Systems analysts begin an assignment by discussing the system's problem with managers and users to determine its exact nature. They then:

- Define the goals of the system and divide the solutions into individual steps and separate procedures.
- Use techniques such as structured analysis, data modeling, information engineering, mathematical model building, and sampling to plan the system.

- Determine what computer hardware and software will be needed to set up a system.
- Coordinate tests and observe initial use of the system to be sure it performs as planned.
- Prepare specifications, work diagrams, and structure charts for computer programmers to follow.
- Work with the programmers to debug errors from the system.

Getting in and moving up. Many employers seek applicants who have a bachelor's degree in computer science, information science, or management information systems (MIS). Management information systems programs are usually part of the business school or college curriculum. These programs differ considerably from computer science programs, emphasizing business- and management-oriented coursework and business computing courses.

Most community colleges and many independent technical schools offer an associate degree in computer science or a related field. Many of these programs may be more geared toward meeting the needs of local businesses and may be more occupation specific than those designed for a 4-year degree. Courses in computer programming or systems design offer good preparation. For jobs in a business environment, employers usually want systems analysts to have business management or closely related skills.

Systems analysts must be able to think logically and have good communication skills. They often deal with a number of tasks simultaneously; the ability to concentrate and pay close attention to detail is important. Systems analysts may be promoted to senior or lead systems analyst. Those who show leadership ability also can become project managers or advance into management positions such as manager of information systems or chief information officer.

Employment forecast and earnings. Computer systems analysts (along with engineers and scientists) are expected to be among the fastest-growing occupations through 2008. In addition, thousands of job openings will arise annually from the need to replace workers who move into managerial positions or other *occupations or who leave the labor force.*

Median annual earnings of computer systems analysts were just over $52,000 in 1998. The lowest 10 percent earned less than $33,000, and the highest 10 percent earned almost $88,000.

Professional connections. The following Web sites provide information about organizations that may be helpful to your job search.

> Institute for Certification of Computing Professionals (ICCP), 2200 East Devon Ave., Suite 268, Des Plaines, IL 60018 http://www.iccp.org
> Institute of Electronic and Electrical Engineers (IEEE), 445 Hoes Lane, Piscataway, NJ 08855   http://wwwieee.org

TECHNICAL WRITERS

What they do.   Technical writers in computer-related industries put scientific and technical information into easily understandable language. They prepare operating and maintenance manuals, catalogs, parts lists, assembly instructions, sales promotion materials, and project proposals. They also plan and edit technical reports and oversee preparation of illustrations, photographs, diagrams, and charts. Technical magazines and hardware companies are located throughout the country, but the largest concentrations are in the Northeast, Texas, and California.

Getting in and moving up.   Technical writing requires a degree in (or at least knowledge about) a specialized field such as engineering, business, or one of the sciences. In many cases, people with good writing skills can learn specialized knowledge on the job. Some transfer from jobs as technicians, scientists, or engineers. Others begin as research assistants or trainees in a technical information department, develop technical communication skills, and then assume writing duties.

For some jobs, the ability to concentrate through confusion and write under pressure is essential. Familiarity with electronic publishing, graphics, and video production equipment is increasingly important.

WHAT KIND OF JOB ARE YOU LOOKING FOR?

Opportunities for advancement can be limited, especially in larger companies where jobs usually are more formally structured than in a small company environment. Beginners generally do research, fact checking, or copyediting. They take on full-scale writing or editing duties less rapidly than do the employees of small companies.

Employment forecast and earnings. The demand for technical writers is expected to increase because of the continuing expansion of scientific and technical information and the need to communicate it to others. In addition to job openings created by employment growth, many openings will occur as experienced workers transfer to other occupations or leave the labor force. Turnover is relatively high in this occupation. Many freelancers leave because they cannot earn enough money.

Median annual earnings for technical writers were about $36,500 in 1998. The lowest 10 percent earned less than $21,000, and the highest 10 percent earned more than $76,500.

Professional connections. The following Web site provides information about organizations that may be helpful to your job search.

Society for Technical Communication, Inc., 901 N. Stuart St., Suite 904, Arlington, VA 22203 http://www.stc-va.org

Software

The collective name given to programs that direct the operation of a computer, or that process electronic data, is *software*. A series of instructions is given to the computer that causes it to do something. The operating system Windows, for example, is known as systems software. Applications programs, usually through a word processor, perform the main tasks.

PROGRAMMERS

What they do. Computer programmers write, test, and maintain the detailed instructions called software, or programs, that computers must

IDENTIFYING THE MATCH: WHAT IT TAKES TO FIT IN

follow to perform their functions. They also conceive, design, and test logical structures for solving problems by computer. Computer programs tell the computer what to do, such as which information to identify and access, how to process it, and what equipment to use. Programs vary widely depending on the type of information to be accessed or generated. For example, the instructions involved in updating financial records are very different from those required to duplicate conditions onboard an aircraft for pilots training in a flight simulator. Although simple programs can be written in a few hours, programs that use complex mathematical formulas or that draw data from many existing systems may require more than a year of work. Usually several programmers work together as a team under a senior programmer's supervision.

Programmers write specific programs by breaking down each step into a logical series of instructions the computer can follow. They then code these instructions in a conventional programming language such as COBOL, or perhaps an artificial intelligence language such as PROLOG, or one of the most advanced function-oriented or object-oriented languages such as Java, C++, or Visual BASIC. Programmers usually know more than one programming language, and since many languages are similar they can often learn new languages relatively easily. Programmers are often referred to by the language they use most, such as Java programmers, or their dominant function or environment, as in database programmers, mainframe programmers, or Internet programmers.

Programmers usually are typecast as either applications programmers or systems programmers, but wireless programmers are on the rise.

- *Applications programmers* usually focus on business, engineering, or science. They write software to handle a specific job, such as a program to track inventory, within an organization. They may also revise existing packaged software.
- *Systems programmers* maintain and control computer systems software such as operating systems, networked systems, and database systems. They make changes in the sets of instructions

that determine how the network, workstations, and central processing unit of the system handle the various jobs they have been given and how they communicate with peripheral equipment, such as terminals, printers, and disk drives. Because of their knowledge of the entire computer system, systems programmers often help applications programmers determine the source of problems that may occur with their programs.
- *Wireless programmers* write programs and code for handheld computers. The imbalance in supply and demand for wireless code writers has headhunters on the lookout and has pushed salaries of some wireless programmers to the highest levels.

Getting in and moving up. The minimum level of education and experience that employers require from programmers has been rising, due to the growing number of qualified applicants and the increasing complexity of some programming tasks. Bachelor's degrees are now commonly required, although some programmers may qualify for certain jobs with 2-year degrees or certificates. College graduates who are interested in changing careers or developing an area of expertise may attend a 2-year community college or technical school for the necessary additional training. Employers seem to be placing more emphasis on previous experience for all types of programmers—even those with degrees. (In 1998, 45.3 percent of working computer programmers had bachelor's degrees.)

Employers using computers for scientific or engineering applications usually prefer college graduates who have degrees in computer or information science, mathematics, engineering, or the physical sciences. Employers who use computers for business applications hire people who have had college courses in management information systems (MIS) and business, preferably with strong programming skills. Increasing emphasis is placed on newer, object-oriented programming languages and tools, such as C++, Visual BASIC, and Java.

Programming jobs call for patience, persistence, and the ability to work on exacting analytical work, especially under pressure.

IDENTIFYING THE MATCH: WHAT IT TAKES TO FIT IN

For skilled workers who keep up-to-date with the latest technology, the prospects for advancement are good. In large organizations, programmers may be promoted to a lead programmer with supervisory responsibilities. Some application programmers may move into systems programming after they take courses in systems software. As employers increasingly contract out programming jobs, more opportunities should arise for experienced programmers with expertise in a specific area to work as consultants. Technical or professional certification is a way to demonstrate an acceptable level of competency.

Employment forecast and earnings. Employment of programmers is expected to grow faster than the average for all occupations through 2008. Jobs for both systems and applications programmers should be plentiful in data processing service firms, software houses, and computer consulting businesses. Employers will continue to need programmers with strong technical skills who understand an employer's business and programming needs. Given the importance of networking and expansion of client/server environments, organizations will look for programmers who can support data communications and help implement electronic commerce and intranet strategies. Market demand for handheld computers has mushroomed and will continue to do so as cellular networks upgrade to third-generation, or 3G, networks, which will allow handheld computers to have always-on online access.

Median annual earnings of computer programmers were about $47,500 in 1998. The lowest 10 percent earned less than $27,000, and the highest 10 percent earned nearly $89,000. As of February 2001, experienced programmers of wireless devices could command annual salaries in excess of $150,000.

Professional connections. The following Web sites provide information about organizations that may be helpful to your job search.

> The WorkSite.Com ("where computer programmers and employers find each other for free") http://www.theworksite.com

WHAT KIND OF JOB ARE YOU LOOKING FOR?

International Programmers Guild (online discussion groups, job and résumé boards, links for programmers) http://www.radionet.com/mail/msg00108.html

Institute for Certification of Computing Professionals (ICCP), 2200 East Devon Ave., Suite 268, Des Plaines, IL 60018 http://www.iccp.org

The Association for Computing Machinery (ACM), 1515 Broadway, New York, NY 10036   http://wwwacm.org

SOFTWARE ENGINEERS

What they do.   Software engineers are involved in the design and development of software systems for control and automation of manufacturing, business, and management processes. They, along with systems analysts who work predominantly with software, oversee the development of new software. A project could involve designing a new application program or other software. (Systems analysts may design either new hardware systems or software products.)

The following are likely steps in designing a new application program:

- *Define the problem.* Discuss the nature of the problem with managers and other users. Through this process, the engineer establishes the goals of the new program so it can be designed to do what users want done.
- *Design the program.* Identify and establish data to be used, input and output files needed, and mathematical and logical operations to be performed; prepare cost-benefit analysis.
- *Determine the sequence of processing.* Engineers and analysts specify the particular files used by the program and design the output to meet users' needs. Other issues include: how the system will function on a network, the security of data, compatibility with existing systems, and design of the user interface.
- *Test and evaluation.* Once the program is written, the engineers and analysts oversee the testing and evaluation process to eliminate as many bugs as possible.

Computer Assisted Software Engineering (CASE) tools are now used extensively to automate much of the programming process, making it easier for a knowledgeable programmer to fill both functions in software development.

Getting in and moving up. Software engineers usually need a bachelor's degree in computer engineering or electrical engineering. A Ph.D. in computer science or engineering—or at least a master's degree—is usually required for jobs in research labs or universities. Employers usually look for people who have broad knowledge and experience in computer systems and technologies, strong problem-solving and analytical skills, and good interpersonal skills. Courses in computer programming or systems design are good preparation for a job in this field.

Computer engineers employed in industry may advance into managerial or project leadership positions. Those in colleges and universities can become heads of research departments or published authorities in their specialty.

Employment forecast and earnings. Computer engineers and scientists are expected to be among the fastest-growing occupations through 2008. Growth will be driven by a highly increasing demand for computer and data processing services, which is projected to be the fastest-growing industry in the U.S. economy.

Median annual earnings of computer engineers were nearly $62,000 in 1998. The lowest 10 percent earned about $37,000, and the highest 10 percent earned almost $93,000.

Professional connections. The following Web site provides information about an organization that may be helpful to your job search.

> Community for Software Engineers ("dedicated to the free information sharing among software engineers")
> http://www.software-engineer.org

INTERFACE DESIGNERS

What they do. Interface designers use human factors engineering, graphic design theory, and other methodologies to design the user interface of a computer system. The user interface is the communication system between the user and the computer. It consists of what you see on the computer screen when you use a program and a set of decisions the designer makes about the interaction. The interface determines how a user is led through a program or process, setting up a likely path or paths for the user to navigate. It also provides a conceptual structure for organizing large amounts of information. Interfaces also offer tools for filtering information and then retrieving it at a later point, according to some set of criteria.

A more specialized branch of interface design is called interaction design. Interaction designers are concerned about the user's experience. They think about how a product feels to a user, how users understand the workings of the product, whether it serves the user's purpose, and how it fits into the entire work context.

Specifically, interface designers:

- Think about the information they want to present and the best way to present it, given what they know about how humans learn and utilize information.
- Create visualizations of an interface concept, usually in the form of sketches.
- Develop storyboards for the interface that include a sequence of elements, the relationships among them, and accompanying scripts.
- Develop working prototypes that give the look and feel of a concept; such prototypes usually work only partially and allow users to try out and "play" with the concept.
- Work with writers and designers to develop the scripts and graphics that will be part of the interface.
- Develop more complete user prototypes that incorporate feedback from the working prototype stage.

- Observe users who are trying out a prototype.
- Complete the interface based on the feedback from the prototype stages.

Interface designers are employed by software development companies, multimedia development firms, research laboratories, design firms, and educational institutions.

Getting in and moving up.   Similar to that of a software engineer.

Employment forecast and earnings.   Similar to that of a software engineer.

New Media

In many ways, the occupations described in this category are not new at all but rather are being applied and adapted in new ways to meet the proliferating and technologically driven needs of Internet and computer-related companies. "New media" affected by this phenomenon include art and design, sound and radio, television and movies, publishing, and, of course, the Internet itself, which combines all of the above.

GRAPHIC DESIGNERS

What they do.   As the graphic design field has expanded, the emphasis has shifted from two-dimensional solutions, such as brochures or posters, to three-dimensional design, including graphics for screen displays. Graphic design can even extend to the creation of physical spaces (such as museum galleries) where a message must be communicated visually. Computer-aided design (CAD) has accelerated the growth of three-dimensional design.

Graphic designers use a variety of print, electronic, and film media to create designs that meet client needs. Most graphic designers use computer software to generate new images. They design promotional displays and marketing brochures for products and services, develop distinctive company logos for products and businesses, and create visual designs of annual reports and other corporate literature. Under the supervision of a design or art director, graphic designers develop the overall layout and design of magazines, newspapers, journals, corporate reports, and other publications. They also develop the graphics and layout of Internet Web sites, and the credits that appear before and after television programs and movies.

Getting in and moving up. Graphic designers must demonstrate artistic ability and creative thinking. Academic training leading to a bachelor's degree in art or design is almost a necessity. Many colleges offer degree programs in fine arts. Art schools also offer postsecondary studio training in the field. Formal educational programs in art and design also provide training in computer techniques. Computers are used widely in the visual arts, and knowledge and training in them are critical for many of the jobs in these fields.

Graphic designers may advance to assistant art director, art director, design director, or creative director of an art or design department. Some graphic designers design Web pages for their company's Internet site. Others open their own businesses and design Web sites on a freelance basis.

Employment forecast and earnings. The visual arts attract many talented people with creative ability, and the number of aspiring graphic designers continues to grow. Therefore, competition for both salaried jobs and freelance work is expected to be keen. Nevertheless, employment of graphic designers and other visual artists is expected to grow faster than the average for all occupations through the year 2008.

Median annual earnings of all visual artists, including graphic designers, were a little under $32,000 in 1998. The lowest 10 percent earned about $18,000, and the highest 10 percent earned almost $65,000.

Professional connections. The following Web site may be helpful to your job search.

IDENTIFYING THE MATCH: WHAT IT TAKES TO FIT IN

The American Institute of Graphic Arts, 164 Fifth Ave., New York, NY 10010 (list of schools offering degree programs; job opportunity board)   http://www.aiga.org

COMPUTER ANIMATORS

What they do. Computer animation is the process of creating moving sequences of pictures (such as cartoons and animated films). Animation can be used to produce entertainment such as movies or video games, as well as for industrial design and scientific research. Four major steps usually are involved:

1. *Storyboarding.* The storyboard provides a visual script for the animation sequence. Usually the storyboard is drawn on paper rather than with the computer. It shows the flow of animation and maps out key scenes and characters.
2. *Modeling.* Modeling is used to convert real objects to animated objects, and to help the animator visualize and control how animated objects will behave in the animation. The real object or physical model is optically scanned by laser and converted to digital form. It can then be viewed and manipulated in three dimensions.
3. *Scripting and movement control.* There are several ways to control movement in animation:
   - Kinematics, which involves animating a model to move according to human patterns of movement.
   - Dynamics, to animate nonhuman objects as though they were real. For example, an animator would use kinematics to animate a human figure but dynamics to animate the movement of the figure's clothing and hair.
   - A combination, where the animator draws both the crucial frames between movements as well as the in-between frames. When the individual cels (or drawings) are photographed, they give the effect of motion. In computer animation, the

WHAT KIND OF JOB ARE YOU LOOKING FOR?

computer can perform calculations to produce the in-between frames, which saves the animator much work.
4. *Rendering.* Rendering is the process of making an object or character appear lifelike by manipulating light, color, texture, and shadow.

Getting in and moving up. Computer animators are best able to enter the field by completing the necessary training at accredited art or design schools. For a list of schools specializing in animation, see the school directory in Animation Magazine at http://www.animationmagazine.net/schools.html.

Employment forecast and earnings. Employment of visual artists, including animators, is expected to grow faster than the average for all occupations through the year 2008. Best locations for animators are the San Francisco Bay Area, Los Angeles, New York City, and Austin, Texas.

According to *Animation Magazine,* salaries for computer animators have skyrocketed in the past few years. Entry-level positions often pay from $40,000 to $65,000. After a few years' experience, skilled animators can make $100,000 or more.

Professional connections. The following Web sites provide information about organizations that may be helpful to your job search.

Digital Media Online, 1508 Brookhollow Dr., Suite 360, Santa Ana, CA http://www.digitalmedianet.com
Animation Magazine, Agoura Hills, CA
http://www.animationmagazine.net
3DSite (worldwide job and message exchange for computer graphics professionals, including animators)
http://www.3dsite.com

DESKTOP PUBLISHERS

What they do. Advances in computer software and printing technology have made it possible to produce on a PC what once took tens of thou-

IDENTIFYING THE MATCH: WHAT IT TAKES TO FIT IN

sands of dollars' worth of complex machinery to accomplish. Desktop publishing (DTP), as this new subindustry is called, continues to change prepress work. Desktop publishing professionals have largely replaced the typesetters, linotype operators, and other workers involved in the prepress process. A projected growth rate of 74 percent and 26,000 new jobs put DTP in the top 10 of the fastest-growing professions.

There are many desktop publishing job titles, some of them overlapping, that employers use to describe the positions they need to fill. When you hear of or see an unfamiliar title that pertains to a DTP opening, find out what responsibilities are required before moving on to the next opportunity. Here are a few titles used by various publishers associated with desktop publishing positions:

- Marketing communications coordinator
- Technical writer
- Technical publications engineer
- Web developer
- Publications engineer
- Digital electronic prepress manager
- Software product manager
- Production supervisor
- Graphic designer
- Documentation specialist
- Digital image processor
- Proofreader
- Training coordinator

Some of the hardware and software skills that employers want their employees to have mastered include Macintosh and related peripherals; MSWord, using templates; Microsoft Office, including PowerPoint and Corel PhotoPaint; QuarkXPress; Illustrator; Harvard Graphics; Corel Ventura; and HTML.

WHAT KIND OF JOB ARE YOU LOOKING FOR?

In addition to the printers and publishers that now hire DTP specialists, more than 4 million self-employed freelancers are working in home-based businesses. Many use the easy-to-use layout software that allows them to produce brochures, newsletters, and even catalogs from their home offices. With their low overhead, such homebound entrepreneurs can compete on an even footing with larger graphic design shops. Those who are skilled writers, of course, are able to reduce their overhead even more. The key usually is to focus on a specific market—health care, real estate, municipal government, or a private educational institution, for example—and meet the unique needs of that market.

Getting in and moving up. For most jobs, a bachelor's or associate's degree is the minimum requirement. It is still possible to train on the job without postsecondary education, but such opportunities grow fewer and fewer. It is also possible to hold either internships or apprenticeships to gain the skills required to do a good job. Workers who exhibit management skills can move on to supervisory positions.

Employment forecast and earnings. Desktop publishing is one of the top 10 fastest-growing occupations projected through 2008, and as such is moving too fast to forecast annual earnings with any accuracy. In general, the average ranges from $15,000 to $60,000—with wide variations from city to city. (See Chapter 12 for information on identifying these variations.)

Professional connections. The following Web sites provide information about organizations that may be helpful to your job search.

> About.com (career information, general and specific)
> http://www.desktoppub.about.com
> DesktopPublishingEzines (includes Web site development, Web designers, links, desktop publishing sources)
> http://desktoppublishing.com/ezine.html

IDENTIFYING THE MATCH: WHAT IT TAKES TO FIT IN

Computer Support

As one of the fastest-growing occupational categories, computer support encompasses a variety of job titles, including help desk specialists, computer repair technicians, network engineers, network and database administrators, hardware and software testers, and computer operators. Computer support specialists assist in activities and operations related to the development and implementation of data processing systems. They also install, test, and document major modifications to systems, procedures, and programs.

SALES AND MARKETING POSITIONS   Looking for your first full-time job in sales and marketing? Trying to leverage brick-and-mortar sales or marketing experience into a dot-com start-up or more established Internet company position? Your best shot is to talk with two or more people who are doing the kind of job you want, research applicable job descriptions on the Web or elsewhere, and plot your strategy accordingly. See Chapter 12 for more information regarding the following job titles—including salary ranges—for your metropolitan area:

- Product managers
- Marketing managers
- Public relations managers
- Sales representatives
- Customer service reps
- Corporate product support managers
- Quality assurance specialists

END USER SUPPORT   An even smoother transition is possible for MIS professionals in conventional companies, or for recently minted business or finance majors who have—as undergrads—made it a point to amass representative hardware and/or software computer skills. Salary and job description information for the following titles also is available in Chapter 12:

WHAT KIND OF JOB ARE YOU LOOKING FOR?

- MIS directors
- Network operations managers
- Information technology analysts
- Installation, maintenance, and repair technicians
- Technical support specialists
- Computer operators
- Data center managers
- Electronic data processing auditors

CHAPTER NINE

Life in the Trenches: Six Professionals Tell Their Stories

So what is it *really* like to work in an Internet or computer-related job?

- Is there a well-defined career path?
- What kind of paycheck can I expect?
- What happens during an average day?
- What are the best and worst parts of the job?
- What kind of person is most likely to succeed?
- How can I get a job like this?

As you might expect, the answers vary widely, depending not only on the job, but on the job seeker as well. And yet, there are some threads of consistency that will help you get a better idea of what awaits—whether you're looking at a dot-com company or a computer-related function in a brick-and-mortar institution.

As you scroll through the portraits of the six professionals profiled in this chapter, your temptation probably will be to look first for the job most like the one you want. This is natural. But don't stop there. Every one of these people has something to say that transcends his or her specialty—and with which you can identify. Read everything in all six profiles, and you'll find useful tips on networking, online job searches, relating to fellow workers, strategies for faster advancement, and preparing sufficiently to get hired in the first place.

RON VICUNEZ—COMPUTER PROGRAMMER IN THE COMMERCIAL BANKING INDUSTRY

Vital Statistics

Experience:	1 year
Education:	Associate degree in computer science. Various technical courses from several institutes and programs. Former naval engineer.
Workweek:	45-plus hours; 8:30 A.M. to 5:30 P.M.
Size of company:	Large regional bank (about 17,000 employees)
Certification:	Range of certifications for various software and systems
Annual salary:	$42,000

What the Job Is Like

What do you do?
I help develop and troubleshoot new online banking applications.

How did you get your job?
After I got out of the Navy, I worked odd jobs—like being a used-car salesman—while taking technical courses and getting different certifications. I got a job programming for a small design firm and stayed there for about a year before beginning my search for something more stable. I actually applied for this job online, took some tests, including a 2-hour exam on Visual BASIC, and then had two rounds of interviews. They called me back, and I got the job.

What are your career aspirations?
In 5 years I'd like to be involved exclusively in developing new applications for customers. I think that's possible. Maybe even sooner than 5 years. My current work gets boring sometimes, and I need more of a challenge. I really have to resist the temptation to change jobs too much, though. It's tempting and very easy because people like me are in such demand right now. I can make a lot more money by changing jobs, but first I think I have to see if this place can take me where I want to go. I think it probably can.

What kinds of people do well in this business?
People who play follow the leader seem to do pretty well. I can do that because I'm used to it from my Navy days, but how well that works for me in the long run I'm not sure yet. Most conversations are work related, and you can't really kid around or even talk about politics. Our city recently had a referendum on a new tax to pay for a professional baseball stadium. The bank supported the tax, but hardly anybody at work wanted to talk about how they felt about it.

What do you really like about your job?
The hours are flexible. I can work 10 hours a day for 4 days if I want to. I also like not sitting at a desk all day, although I hate coming back to a cubicle. Guys on my level don't have to wear a coat and tie, although some do wear a tie. I don't.

What do you dislike?
The corporate culture. It's pretty straightlaced, and I am not crazy about that. But I'm getting used to it. People are strictly business. There is very little interaction on a lighthearted or even semipersonal level. But neither is the culture overbearing nor intimidating, and the bank encourages and rewards creativity and teamwork. My supervisor is more of a banking type than any of the people on my level. He wears a jacket and tie and deals with the senior executives in the bank. I don't have much official contact with them.

IDENTIFYING THE MATCH: WHAT IT TAKES TO FIT IN

What is the biggest misconception about this job?
I think many noncomputer people think you have to be a brainiac to have this job, but you don't. Most of the stuff I do, at least right now, is pretty basic in terms of what programmers do. Hopefully, that will change.

How can someone get a job like yours?
People come here from all backgrounds. Some of the top programmers have a college degree and some don't. People learn about openings from others in the field or through the Internet. The important thing is how well you do on the technical tests. A degree may influence your promotion, but you can usually get a job if you show that you know your stuff.

Ron's Typical Day

6:30   Get up. Feed the dog, turn on the juicer, and make carrot and orange juice for me and my wife. I'm not big on breakfast.

7:30   Out the door.

8:15   Arrive and check my e-mail.

8:30   In our group, programmers work in teams of three, so we usually try to meet briefly when the day begins to discuss what we've got ahead of us.

9:30   The biggest part of my job is making sure that the people who bank from home, as well as corporate bankers, can access the system with no trouble. My first task each day is to see that the system is responding quickly and efficiently. I also have to check for unauthorized users. If there are no problems, then I move on to the customer service enhancements we're working on.

11:00   Spend some time with a program to install dialup networking on customers' computers. This is a programming job, but one that's very closely connected to our customers. If they don't like or want the new features we're developing, we need to pay attention and make changes in what we're doing. Right now I'm immersed in some of these new changes.

12:00 Lunch, usually in the employee cafeteria with team members. We talk mostly about work. All of the guys are real computer nerds, the only difference is that some really look like nerds and others don't.

1:00 More work on the dialup networking program. It takes almost as long to make a few changes as it does to develop something from scratch. Because it's a bank, everything has to be checked and checked again and then checked a few more times.

2:00 Shift my attention to a problem one of my team members is working on. He and I are actually working on it together. We discuss our progress and write up what still needs to be done. Banks not only need perfect QA (quality assurance) but also clear timelines and progress updates.

3:00 Back to the dialup networking program. The current task is to teach the application to recognize passwords and numbers, which means lots of experimentation at this point.

5:10 Off to the parking lot and the baby Benz for the trip home.

TYRONE YOUNG—QUALITY ASSURANCE ENGINEER IN THE COMPUTER SOFTWARE INDUSTRY

Vital Statistics

Age: 29
Experience: $1\frac{1}{2}$ years
Education: B.S., Computer Science; J.D.
Work week: 50 hours; 10:30 A.M. to 8:30 P.M., plus whatever time I want for lunch

> ## When You Are Part of a Team—Temporarily
>
> The 3.3 million temporary workers in the United States now have a way to share the boredom, invisibility, and dispensability that goes with the territory: Web sites. One of them, Temp NYC (www.tempnyc.com) warns, "Be prepared to be ignored." The site teaches temps to cover their tracks while surfing the Internet and offers other tips, such as eating the limit and stocking up on drinks if a company pays for meals, or the basics of assembling a simple mix-and-match wardrobe. "I wore the same tie at one job for four months straight, and nobody said a word," one advice-giver wrote. "Remember, you are invisible."
>
> Another site, Temp 24/7 (www.temp24-7.com) includes regular features such as Temp Tales of Horror and Gripe of the Week. The Administrative Resources Network (www.adresnet.com), a site for administrative assistants, offers advice when dealing with temp agencies. Some agencies often advertise interesting—but unavailable—jobs to build up a staff list, the site warns, and shunt overqualified candidates off to jobs that are beneath them. They sometimes also offer "full benefits" that are extremely difficult to retrieve.
>
> —Daniel J. Wakin
> Adapted from the *New York Times*

Size of company: 140 employees
Certification: None
Annual salary: $50,000, plus medical, dental, vision, 10 paid vacation days, 2 mental health days, 10 or so holidays, and free food

What the Job Is Like

What do you do?
I develop test plans for online software in order to make it easy for people to create their own Web pages. This entails anticipating what can go

wrong with the product before it goes through thorough testing. I have to pretend I'm an average user—"black box" testing—and examine the code for loopholes in logic—"white box" testing. I work with the systems, development, and production departments to ensure that new releases of the software go smoothly, and with few bugs.

What did you do previous to this?
I was an editor, working on electronic products and examining them for content.

How did you get your job?
I looked on the Internet for Web sites that needed QA engineers and developers.

What are your career aspirations?
To be able to construct a Web site from the ground up, coding through systems.

What kinds of people do well in this business?
People in this business should be detail-oriented and technically savvy. You should be able to figure out how to change the time on your car or stereo without reading the manual. You should be a good problem solver with a good memory. Never settle into your own job, and strive to do more than your job. Learn what people around you are doing. When you're working in quality assurance, talk to people in development and systems. Make them explain why things work the way they do. It makes you a better tester and more useful in general. In a healthy, growing company, no one will think you are taking their job; they'll be thrilled that someone else will know what to do while they are on vacation.

What do you really like about your job?
I like the flexibility and the fact that I have lots of room to grow.

What do you dislike?
I dislike when the job starts to overtake my life—when I start to spend more than 55 hours a week at work, my social life suffers.

What is the biggest misconception about this job?
The biggest misconception is that it is not a technical position. Quality assurance engineers are very valuable, and it's very useful to have some development skills when applying for a QA engineer position.

Looking back on your career or job search, what do you wish you had done differently?
Honestly, I've been pretty happy with my major choices.

How can someone get a job like yours?
Search the Internet for companies that interest you—each site usually has a jobs section. If you apply directly instead of through a service, you seem more genuinely interested in the company. (And it shows you've looked at their Web site.)

Tyrone's Typical Day

10:30 Get to work.
11:00 Meet with producers to discuss upcoming projects.
12:00 Meet with developers to discuss current software problems.
1:00 Get lunch.
2:00 Test specific areas of our site.
3:00 Change some server settings on our testing machines to optimize performance.
5:00 Research a new technology to enhance our product development and testing environments.
7:00 Research third-party software for possible bugs, which may be influencing our product's performance.
8:30 Go home.

MARK WHISLER—SOFTWARE TECHNICAL WRITER

Vital Statistics

Age: 44
Experience: 6 years as a technical writer, 10 years of editorial experience
Education: A.A. degree; 1 year toward B.A.
Workweek: 40 to 65 hours
Size of company: 500 employees
Certification: None
Annual Salary: $45,000 to $50,000

What the Job Is Like

What do you do?
I oversee the production of user manuals for computer games. I write them, edit them, and manage their layout. I interface with various groups that input content for the user manuals. I deal with the marketing department for the art, with R&D for functionality, with the fulfillment house for production, and with design contractors to get the layout done. I interface with the legal department to make sure the legal stuff is correct. Through my department, we produce between 15 and 20 manuals each year, ranging from 25 pages to 220 pages each.

I'm the sole technical writer at my company. I do have a couple of contractors, but I manage all of it.

What did you do previous to this?
I was an editor at a database company. I edited records for inclusion in a periodical database.

How did you get your job?
A friend told me that there was an opening at a computer game company. It seemed more interesting than what I was doing, so I decided to go for it.

IDENTIFYING THE MATCH: WHAT IT TAKES TO FIT IN

What are your career aspirations?
I'm getting ready to leave this job and work for a different company. I want to continue to refine my craft and make more money.

What kinds of people do well in this business?
People who are dedicated to creating quality product and who have good English skills and a good level of attention to detail do well. You have to be a self-starter and know that you can't rely on people to provide what they promised. You have to be willing to go out and get it. At a different company, where there's a full staff of technical writers, that might be a different story, but here where I work, I have to be self-motivated.

What do you really like about your job?
I like that I'm unsupervised and I set my own hours. Also, I get to play all the games!

What do you dislike?
I dislike doing the same kinds of things over and over. Since I'm the only guy who does what I do, and since I do it as well as I do, they have come to rely on me too much to let me try my hand at other types of work.

What is the biggest misconception about this job?
The biggest misconception is that it's easy, that there's not a lot of work involved, and that anybody who can string a sentence together could do it.

Looking back on your career or job search, what do you wish you had done differently?
I don't really have any regrets in terms of things that I had any control over.

How can someone get a job like yours?
It's helpful to have an editorial background. You have to prove you've got the ability to write well. Also, look for internships. Approach companies you like and ask if they're interested in hiring someone in a technical writing role. A lot of companies just don't hire technical writers.

Look at the kind of work you want to do and practice it. For example, if you've ever played a game that had a terrible manual, try writing a better one. Being able to demonstrate what you can do is extremely impressive. There are also technical writing programs in a lot of local universities, but they're not necessarily aimed at the gaming industry. You could also join the Society for Technical Communication—it's basically a trade organization for technical writers. They offer job listings, training, and peer groups.

Mark's Typical Day

9:00   I get into the office and check my e-mail and voice mail messages. The messages are typically queries about where a particular job is, responses to queries I've made about material people owe me, or requests for archival materials from manuals we've done in the past.

10:00   I prioritize which tasks I need to be working on based on how quickly they're going to be needed for layout, how soon they need to go to press, and when they need to be delivered to R&D for their review. I might spend most of my day editing, but I also spend time chasing people down to make sure they deliver.

12:00   I have lunch in our company cafeteria.

1:30   I have two midafternoon meetings each week. One is a production meeting where the R&D staff talks about the status of our projects. The other is an R&D group meeting where R&D managers and supervisors talk about any problems and company news that we might have.

4:00   I go back to my projects. In addition to writing and editing, I do a lot of graphic manipulation. The screen shots that go in the user manuals are generally captured by technical writers.

6:00   I make sure the most recent version of the document I've been working on has been saved. Then I might look at what I need to do the next day and leave myself a reminder like "Don't forget to do this!" I usually go home between 6:00 and 6:30. On a busier day, I might be here until midnight.

JAY WARD—DIRECTOR OF BUSINESS DEVELOPMENT, INTERNET & NEW MEDIA

Vital Statistics

Age:	36
Experience:	2 years
Education:	B.A., political science, Williams College; J.D., Harvard Law School
Workweek:	70 hours
Size of company:	70 employees
Certification:	None
Annual salary:	$110,000, plus end-of-year bonus and stock options

What the Job Is Like

What do you do?
I'm the director of business development for a company that creates B2B, industry-specific search engines for vertical Web sites that focus on a particular industry or subject matter. I manage and lead our business development team in the creation and management of partnership relationships. I identify potential partners and negotiate co-branding and licensing deals with them. Because I joined my company at an early stage, I have also been involved in building the infrastructure and processes of the business development department.

How did you get your job?
By networking. I wanted to move into Internet business development so I took a class on start-up operations through UC Berkeley. There I

met a consultant who was affiliated with the company that I work for now.

What are your career aspirations?
In the short term I want to become a vice president of business development at a company where I can run a larger business development team and have more authority. My long-term goal is to become the CEO of a company in 2 to 4 years. In order to do this, I'll need to build up a strong network for contacts in the venture capital and the broader Internet communities. The Internet space is so fluid right now I don't really know what type of company I'd like to run, but it will definitely be in a high-growth area.

What kinds of people do well in this business?
To do well in Internet business development you need an equal mix of technical and industry knowledge. Specifically, the following skills are important: relationship identification, account management, and client development; understanding the legal framework of deals and being comfortable in deal negotiation; being good at contract preparation and analysis; and having a fundamental understanding of the product and services that your company provides. Few people enter business development with all these skills, which is why experience is so essential.

What do you really like about your job?
Doing deals. When I was a kid I loved Monopoly. I couldn't wait to reach the point in the game when a deal had to be done because whichever player got the better end of the deal would win the game. I also like the fact that strategic alliances and acquisitions are key to creating value in an Internet business.

What do you dislike?
The lack of control. A business development executive is a diplomat, not a general. Our job is to build bridges and establish relationships. I can never tell an engineer what product to build, and I can't tell a partner what terms to accept. I have to juggle the interests of the marketing team,

the engineers, the finance people, partners, and partners' lawyers. My joy is all about building relationships in order to cut the best deal possible for my company.

What is the biggest misconception about this job?
Some people mistakenly believe that understanding technology is not necessary to be successful. To succeed you need to know how technology connects to the overall business goals of your company. No matter what your company does, there will always be an engineer on the other side who can kill a deal. You must be able to address engineers' objections and communicate business development's objectives to them.

Many people also get into business development thinking it's more strategy than sales. This is not always the case. At the moment, the Internet is suffering from serious deal inflation, and in many cases what is in actuality a sale is often reported as a strategic alliance or a partnership.

One way to find out if a business development job is going to involve more sales than strategy is to look at the title of the position you are applying for. If the title is business development manager, it's likely to be more sales-oriented. If the title is vice president of business development, the position will probably involve more strategy. VPs tend to play more of a role in the direction of the company and building up strategic alliances and partnerships.

Looking back on your career or job search, what do you wish you had done differently?
I wish I'd gotten into the industry earlier. There is a significant lack of talent and depth of people who can do deals and do them well. People who have lots of experience negotiating and who have built up a good Rolodex will be in high demand.

How can someone get a job like yours?
Network. Networking is huge in this industry. If you live in the Bay Area, I recommend attending the Internet Business Development Forum. The IBDF is an organization that I recently founded. The forum

meets once a month, and there are 50 to 60 business development representatives at the meetings. You should also make calls to small, growing Internet companies. After a company gets its first or second round of funding, it hires business development executives to make deals. Keep your eye out for companies that have recently received funding.

Jay's Typical Day

6:30   Arrive at the office. Check to see if I have any urgent e-mail from the East Coast. Grab a bagel and read the *San Jose Mercury News* business section to see if any new deals have been announced or if there are any major personnel announcements. Doing deals is a lot easier if you have a contact at the company. I always keep an eye out to see where people I know have gone to work.

7:00   Prepare for business development team meeting. Rework a PowerPoint presentation about my team's priorities for the coming months. Review an Excel spreadsheet on traffic stats from our site.

8:00   Attend business development team meeting. Review existing deals we have in place. Go through our priorities for the coming weeks. The meeting ends with a presentation from the head of our marketing department. She discusses new features and product developments that are in the works.

9:00   Prepare for an 11:00 meeting with a potential partner. Most of my day is spent creating new partner relationships or managing and attending to relationships that already exist. I usually have anywhere between 3 and 12 deals or projects in the works. In preparing for the meeting I try to anticipate any product requirements that this potential partner may have. That way, when they ask about certain capabilities in the meeting, I'll know whether we can meet their needs. I also list the resources that we bring to the table for a potential partner. The list helps me measure the total value of the services we are offering.

11:00 Meet with the potential partner. They are definitely interested: we just need to figure out where our logo is going to be located on the partner's Web site and how quickly we can deploy our search engine on their site. The deployment depends on how quickly the engineers can do the work that is needed.

2:00 Evaluate the performance of an existing partnership that we have. I analyze the Web site traffic data from the last month that the partnership has been in place. I need to figure out how we can get more traffic or revenue from the relationship. This might involve changing the placement of our service on their Web site.

4:00 Work with lawyers on a contract that we are finalizing. Respond to requests for information.

6:00 Finish writing and drafting contracts and completing reports on traffic and deal terms.

7:30 Have a drink with a friend before heading home.

ARNOLD DUBOIS—WEB DEVELOPER, INTERNET & NEW MEDIA

Vital Statistics

Age: 23
Experience: 1 1/2 years
Education: B.A., philosophy, Stanford University
Workweek: 55 hours
Size of company: 50 employees
Certification: None
Annual Salary: $55,000

What the Job Is Like

What do you do?
My company provides the technology that allows major online portals and e-business firms to offer Internet access, e-mail service, and that sort of thing. I work on the back end of the system—the programming and coding part, mostly—that integrates our service with our customers' databases.

How did you get your job?
As a philosophy major, I knew it was going to be difficult earning a living in my chosen field. I took a couple of programming classes, and after I graduated, I took a job as a programmer at a financial services firm. It wasn't exactly my crowd, so when a friend told me about the job at this company, I interviewed and decided to take it.

What are your career aspirations?
I like what I do, but I'm not passionate about programming. Eventually I'd like to be a philosophy teacher.

What kinds of people do well in this business?
People who can take a task and run with it. People who work well independently. This position would not be ideal for someone who needs structure.

What do you really like about your job?
The people are all young and laid-back—and a lot of fun. There aren't office politics. Being independent and taking initiative is encouraged. I also like the fact that my work is tangible. A page on a site goes up, and I can say, "Look, Mom. I did that."

What do you dislike?
I'm not fascinated by the Internet. I'm interested in it, but I just don't share that same sense of captivation that a lot of people here have. In that way, I feel a little bit like I'm on the sidelines of the adventure.

What is the biggest misconception about this job?
I guess the biggest surprise has been how much independence I've been given. My hours are fairly flexible, as long as I put in the time and make

sure my projects get done. Maybe people don't realize how much freedom there is.

Looking back on your career or job search, what do you wish you had done differently?
I probably should have networked more before I graduated. I wish I could have started at a place like this, rather than waste time at a company—in my case, a financial services firm—that wasn't really a fit.

How can someone get a job like yours?
Network with friends. Learn programming skills. Make sure you come across as someone who learns quickly and adapts easily.

Arnold's Typical Day

- 10:00 Check and respond to e-mail. Review yesterday's work.
- 11:00 Meet with our in-house designers about beginning a new project: implementing a sign-up process for a partner who wants to offer free e-mail service. Our designers create the system, and I make it work.
- 12:00 Begin the process of writing up and coding the program, integrating information our partner provides with our technology. This means parsing the info—in this case, the statistics our partner wants to gather about the people signing up for its Internet service—and storing it in a database.
- 3:00 Lunch with a buddy from the office.
- 4:00 Weekly staff meeting. First we introduce all the new hires—our company has almost doubled in size since October, when I came on board. Then we talk about new clients, what their needs are, and how we'll go about serving them.
- 5:00 Make sure the pages that were launched last week are working properly. If there are glitches, I need to scour the

code or check with other Web servers to determine where the problem is.
7:00 Call it a day.

RUBY GONZALES—PRODUCER, INTERNET & NEW MEDIA

Vital Statistics

Experience: 2½ years
Education: B.A., art history
Workweek: 50 to 70 hours, usually 8:00 A.M to 6:30 P.M.
Size of company: 51 employees
Annual salary: $45,000 plus stock options, which after 4 years at the company will be worth anywhere from nothing (if the company goes out of business) to $100,000 or more

What the Job Is Like

What do you do?
I work for a company that runs an online store. I'm responsible for the Web site and the products sold there. I also coordinate the work of the engineering, design, and marketing teams.

What did you do previously?
I was an administrative assistant at a small publishing company.

How did you get your job?
When I came to work here, there were only eight people in the company, so they wanted someone who could do a lot of different things—administration, operations, marketing, and so forth—and who could learn on the fly and grow with the company. So I basically showed that I had project management skills and that I was smart and easily adaptable. As the

company has grown, the projects that have come my way have become more complex, I've assumed more responsibility, and my salary has increased.

What are your career aspirations?
I really don't know. I'd say there's a 25 percent chance I'll still be in this industry in 5 years. The industry track for me would be to get my MBA, then get a job in online business development, then move into a senior management role. But I think I'd rather get a Ph.D. in art history and teach at a liberal arts college.

What kinds of people do well in this business?
Outgoing people who communicate well. At this company, everybody knows the big picture: Marketing people have ideas about what engineering should be doing, and engineers have ideas about what marketing should be doing. If you're not outgoing or don't communicate well, you'll have a hard time getting into the loop. You'll also need initiative and flexibility to handle the lack of structure. There won't always be someone to tell you what to do, and things can change quickly. And it's definitely fast-paced and high-stress, so you need to cope well with stress.

What do you really like about your job?
I like that I can go barefoot in the office. It's a very warm, human environment. I like that the management structure is egalitarian, with a strong sense of mutual trust. And the people I work with are very smart and dynamic. I'm constantly learning.

What do you dislike?
In such a volatile industry, there's a realistic chance that any small company will go out of business. That means there are times when things get pretty bleak and very stressful. And sometimes I feel like this whole company is extraneous, that what we're doing doesn't matter.

What is the biggest misconception about this job?
That everyone makes a million dollars. Most people don't.

How can someone get a job like yours?
As the Web matures, we're seeing more candidates with previous Web experience. So any Web experience—including internships—is valuable. But it's definitely not a prerequisite. More important is that a person be a good fit—comfortable with an egalitarian, unstructured work environment and a frequently changing job description. Beyond that, one thing that differentiates candidates is their knowledge of our company and our competitors. A candidate who has spent a few hours surfing our site and our competitors' sites and who comes in with a few thoughtful things to say about the landscape is way ahead of most other candidates who come through here.

Ruby's Typical Day

8:30 Come in, fire up both computers (one Mac, one PC). Deal with 27 e-mails spread across three accounts—the CEO has a new idea for the site, an engineer wants to push back the work schedule on our commerce overhaul, a friend is having a dinner party, and so on....

9:00 Meet with a designer and a copywriter to make sure they're on track in their work on our upcoming page redesign.

10:15 Walk down to the bay and back. It's a clear, cold day.

10:30 Interview a candidate for a design position we have. We're hiring so fast these days that interviewing is like a part of life. She's done some good work, but I'm not sure she can handle the pace here.

11:30 Put together a quarterly report for one of our strategic partners. Analyze impressions, click-throughs, and sales for the traffic that came from its site to ours. Actually, dealing with partnerships is not in my job description anymore, but I'm maintaining some of the relationships while the guy who's taken over that responsibility gets up to speed.

IDENTIFYING THE MATCH: WHAT IT TAKES TO FIT IN

12:45 Tuna sandwich in South Park.

1:10 Surf our competitors' sites to see if they're up to anything new. Nothing earth-shattering today.

2:00 Run some numbers through Excel to try and figure out the data from our most recent promotion.

3:30 E-mail backlog: 13. Uh-oh. Busy, busy, busy.

4:00 Meet with the engineer who's on the commerce overhaul. Tell him we can't push back the launch date. Agree 5 minutes later to push back the launch date by a week.

5:00 Write a long e-mail to the CEO detailing my ideas for integrating the e-commerce overhaul and the Web site redesign. Add a note explaining my analysis of the data from the recent promotion.

5:45 Spend a while thinking through some long-term strategic issues. Sometimes it doesn't seem like we'll ever be profitable....

6:15 Do some beta testing of the e-commerce overhaul. Find some bugs, but have an idea to improve the interface. E-mail the relevant engineer.

7:00 Shut down. Out the door.

PART FOUR

Getting the Job You Want

To effectively apply all you now know about the Internet and the various kinds of companies that inhabit it, use it, service it, and rely on it, certain skills are essential. You'll be competing for opportunities not only with other accomplished specialists who want to move into this new terrain but also with veteran dot-com and Web company professionals who know the turf and will use this familiarity to their advantage.

CHAPTER TEN

Marketing Brand You: What to Do with Your Targeted Résumé

A well-written résumé is still the most important piece of self-promotion any professional on the move can own. If a prospective employer doesn't know you, a good résumé—or, under some circumstances, a good letter of introduction—is essential to getting an interview. If you don't see your potential boss face-to-face, you're not going to get the job. It's as simple as that.

As to the document itself, the only effective résumé is one that leads to interviews. The résumés you will see in this book—and the one you will learn to write—are designed to generate interviews.

If you're responding to an advertisement, or otherwise hear about an opening that is known to other candidates, your competition can be anywhere from a dozen to several hundreds of others who want the job, depending on the size of the company and the aggressiveness of the staffing department. Under these circumstances, and considering that a first reader is your make-or-break judge to winnow the stack of résumés to a manageable few, your fate at that company may be decided in 30 seconds or less. Before each résumé reader is a list of keywords and phrases to be matched against specific skills, experiences, or accomplishments. If you don't hit three out of five (or four out of five, wherever the bottom line has been drawn), you won't make the first cut.

If you're making a cold call on a company—either because you know of an opening or because your capabilities and experience qualify you for an opportunity you've heard is likely to break—a strong résumé is the tool you need to get in the door.

First-time job seekers—college grads, for the most part—are judged slightly differently, although no less rigorously. The company's first readers (or in smaller companies, your boss-to-be) will look closely at your grades and the way you spent your summers, rather than at your experience and professional accomplishments. Internships and career-related volunteer work rank very high in the eyes of most employers.

But no matter what your level or specialty, your intended end product will be the same: a résumé that communicates totally and instantly.

WRITING FOR SPECIFIC AUDIENCES

All successful résumés are written with a specific audience in mind. Writing successfully to an employer's needs will depend on the mastery of three essential levels of information:

- Knowledge of industry
- Knowledge of company
- Knowledge of position or function

The simplest, most easily managed goal is to move up the ladder in a relatively straight line, taking on more or broader responsibilities in both your function and industry. Here your job is to demonstrate an awareness of industry trends, problems, and promise. If you are coming from a non-Internet company, emphasize any IT-related skills, accomplishments, and responsibilities that are transferable to Net company needs.

The best way to communicate effectively is to write a résumé targeted to a specific situation. First prepare a master résumé that you can adjust as you need to. By researching what your targeted employers want from a candidate (Web sites first, library directories second) you will learn what is important to them. Structure your résumé to make it easy for an employer to see the most relevant skills and accomplishments. This will both increase your prospective employer's comfort level with you and make it easier to visualize you doing the job.

In these days of virtual universal PC ownership, making small changes to accommodate a particular situation is a simple task. In most instances, such changes need to be made in the objective and summary sections only. Occasionally an adjustment is called for in the experience section as well. Substitute an accomplishment or responsibility—or revise the sequence—to match the needs of today's opening. This is all minor tinkering.

RÉSUMÉ FORMATTING

The elegant, watermarked, 20-pound ivory-tinted paper you used for your standard résumé will be of little use when you apply for a job electronically. You'll want to save copies of this one for your interviews, naturally, but to compete successfully in the Internet job hunt you'll need at least one more version. It must be tailored and formatted for online job opportunities, where a prospective employer, recruiter, or online job service will see it.

Electronic résumés can be submitted in several different ways: via e-mail or online, in either an ASCII or a scannable format. If you e-mail résumés, remember that most e-mail programs wrap anything longer than 72 characters over to the next line. So keep your line length under this limit to avoid an amateurish and distracting appearance. To give you an idea:

This line, including all letters, commas, and spaces, has 71 characters

Submit e-mail résumés as part of the message rather than as an attachment, unless you are requested otherwise. Many companies are spooked by résumé attachments and won't bother to open them.

ASCII Text

ASCII is a common text language that allows different word processing applications to read and display the same information. ASCII stands for American Standard Code for Information Interchange and describes files that are stored in clear text format. It is the simplest form of text and is not platform- or application-specific. To accommodate this, there is no formatting mechanism within the text.

Because ASCII text does not recognize special formatting commands, there is little need to think about white space or other stylistic niceties—or even the modest use of such typographic devices as bullets, underlines, and italics. Here are a few other rules to remember:

- Avoid using special characters such as mathematical symbols; they will not be accurately transferred.
- Do not use tabs, for the same reason. Use the space bar instead.
- The default alignment for ASCII is everything left justified. To indent a sentence or center a heading, use the space bar.
- Do not use the word wrap feature when typing your résumé; instead, use hard carriage returns to insert line breaks.
- Because fonts become whatever your computer uses as its default typeface and size, boldface, italics, and sizes other than the default size will not be recognized.

Scannable Résumés

To get read online, scannable résumés have to pass the OCR (optical character recognition) test. Those of you with scanners can translate what you've written in a way that allows the computer to read and understand it. There are also a few rules specific to scannable résumés:

- Typeface should be between 10 and 12 points. (*The Dot-Com Decision* is set in 11.5 point type.)
- Use a sans serif rather than a serif typeface. A serif is the tail at the end of parts of some letters—as in the "feet" at the bottom of capital "A." Sans serif (without serifs) is cleaner and easier to read than a serif face. Examples of sans serif typefaces include Optima, Univers, and Futura.
- Boldface type and words in capital letters are okay for section headings and emphasis, as long as the letters don't touch each other.
- Stay away from underlining and italics. They may not scan accurately.
- If you use bullets, include a space after each.
- Avoid parentheses, brackets, and compressed lines of type.
- Avoid tabs and hard carriage returns whenever possible.
- Use keywords (nouns, rather than verbs) to list all your skills and strengths. Scanners search résumés for keywords and then file them under the appropriate categories. Most of you with backgrounds in information technology are used to listing all the hardware, software, and platforms with which you are familiar (perhaps grouped just under your objective and summary). Use multiple synonyms for the same skills to be sure your qualifications are picked up. All of you in related functions (for example, new media or desktop publishing) should similarly work up those keywords that best capture your strengths.

The résumé is scanned into the system, and the computer then reads it. Type your name at the top of the page. Then, on their own lines, add your address in the standard format, followed by your phone and fax numbers. Section headings should be boldface or capitalized. Keep copies of your more polished-looking print résumé for interviewers, after your electronic résumé has done its job, which is to get you the interview in the first place.

SUBMITTING YOUR RÉSUMÉ ONLINE

Now, using the key that opens up the hundreds of job-search possibilities inside those electronic portals, which version of your online-friendly résumé do you use? "I always prepare ASCII résumés with the scanner in mind," says Sheila Brackenbury, a Vermont Web site developer. "Often those companies that ask for an ASCII will scan it anyway, so this way you can write one version to fit both kinds of situations. Some of the firms we've dealt with online will say, 'Send us your ASCII and attach your Word (or WordPerfect) document.' So you send them the plain one; they'll quickly scan through it for keywords or whatever, and then they've got the nice Word doc to keep on file."

"Most of the bigger job-posting sites," says Brackenbury, "MonsterBoard and HotJobs, for example—and others, I'm sure—will walk you through the process. Some of them have online forms you can fill out. At the JobBank in Vermont, job seekers write résumés from the print versions they have in front of them. So you don't post an ASCII document, you write it online."

Many of the newer Internet companies seem not to be as good about acknowledging receipt of résumés as their brick-and-mortar brethren. It may be that inquiries received by computer rather than by mail contribute to a dehumanization of the process, where a signed letter somehow makes the candidate seem more "real." It may also be that in a young dot-com, a candidate-sensitive human resource department is rarely a vital concern. In any case, be prepared for a lower rate of response when applying to dot-com start-ups.

Inside View

Kelly Irish, Boston College Student

As a graduate of Boston College's class of 2001, Kelly Irish spent a good portion of her senior year researching and interviewing for her first full-time, permanent job—while at the same time making good enough grades for the dean's list, and completing an internship with a Boston area incubator. With a B.S. in information systems, Kelly wasn't certain exactly what her role in IT would be, or what she wanted it to be.

Q How did you come to choose your major?

A I wanted to combine my interest for computers with a business management degree. An information systems program satisfied those interests and will give me a strong background that will come in handy for a variety of jobs. Also, it seemed to me that there would be good career opportunities for a student with an information systems degree.

Q Have you thought about a specialty?

A It's tricky to decide on a specialty so early. While I do have some experience, I don't have enough to really understand any specific job. If I had to choose, I'd say it would be in the area of electronic commerce or perhaps as a business analyst.

Q In your queries to prospective employers, have you been that specific or have you been talking more generally?

A More general. I'm not 100 percent sure what I want to do. Also, job titles differ from company to company, so I'm still not sure about the terminology. For the most part I'm exploring companies that interest me to see what they offer students just coming out of college.

Q I see by your résumé that you interned at Cargill. What kind of experience did that give you?

A What I realized with my experience at Cargill was that I needed to have a strong connection with the industry. I just didn't connect to the agricultural food industry. Also, I was in an area of the company that

continued on next page

was too technical for me. I was surrounded by programmers—people who were on the technical side. In my major there's a technical route and an analyst route. I learned that I was happier on the analyst side.

Q *So, you've ruled out the food industry and the technical side. How else have you arranged your priorities for the kind of company and kind of job you want?*

A Well, it's really hard to know. In school if I didn't like a class, after a semester I never had to deal with it again. In a job I will have to commit a lot of time to both the position and the company, so I want to find the best fit possible: Will I like the tasks that I would have to perform every day, what does the job have to do with my interests, and will I like the company and what it is involved in?

Q *Information interviewing—without the risks of a "live" interview—can help in this way. Do you do any of that?*

A Yes. I've found a few companies that I was interested in and identified contacts within them so that I could sit down with them and ask about the company, what they liked and didn't like about it, and what the people around them were doing. I also told them what I was interested in and asked if there were jobs at the company that had any correlation with my interests. Sometimes this has led me to job titles I never knew existed, so I've been able to identify the people who held those jobs and talk to them.

Q *What are some other investigative tactics you've used?*

A Oh, family, friends, friends of friends, contacts through my school, career fairs. At our career center we can access the alumni network, which is a database of alumni willing to meet with students to discuss careers and help with job leads. I also use Web sites like Monster.com to research companies and job descriptions.

Q *Do you use your career center regularly?*

A I'm one of the few lucky people to have developed a relationship with a specific counselor, which helps a lot. I can go in and practice inter-

continued on next page

viewing and get my résumé critiqued. I can also use the electronic recruiting system from the career center's Web site, through which students can apply for jobs that recruiters have posted on campus. This is really convenient because everything can be done electronically from my dorm room.

Q What has been most surprising in your search?
A I didn't realize how long it would take or how complicated it would be. The number of companies out there—pretty soon you're on information overload. You have to allot a few hours several times a week to research, make contacts, and schedule interviews. I also get e-mails all the time from companies that say they will be on campus, or from job-search Web sites I've subscribed to. One thing that frustrates me is that many times I just want to talk to people about their jobs, their career path, and any advice they may have for me. But people seem to think I'm trying to use them to get a job at that company, so they conduct themselves differently than just having a conversation with me.

Q How long have you been at this?
A I've been thinking about what kind of work I'd like to do after graduation since my sophomore year. I used to set up meetings with my academic advisor and try to define the ideal job and companies with which I could intern during the summer. Now that I'm a senior, I'm still looking for the ideal job. A lot of people just take a job rather than look into a career. My advisor at the career center told me that there are people who take the first job offered to them and are back in the career center within a year to start the process all over again.

Q Back to your résumé. Do you have two versions?
A I just have one. But sometimes I find a problem with those Internet submissions. At Monster.com, for example, they require users to enter little bits and pieces of their résumé at a time instead of uploading the résumé all at once. A lot of companies have their own little submission

continued on next page

boxes, or they may have an easier cut-and-paste window, rather than sending the résumé as an uploaded document.

Q *Does it sometimes end up looking weird?*
A If you use the entry boxes they provide on the Web site, there's no problem. I'm more concerned about whether someone will actually look at my résumé or if it will just go straight to a database. Many times a résumé is left in a database until someone does a specific search for certain keywords in the document. This isn't always helpful for someone looking for a job. I feel more confident when I send my résumé to an actual person's e-mail address, rather than a generic HR address found on a company Web site or through a job-search portal such as Monster.com.

Q *Have you changed the way you go about this since September, when you started?*
A In September I was looking for a job description that I liked—what roles and responsibilities I wanted to have—but that wasn't narrow enough. Right now I'm looking at four companies, but with this new strategy I'm a little nervous about not giving myself enough options.

Q *How have you developed your interviewing skills?*
A First of all, I try to set up an information interview. This way I get background information on the company so that if I interview with someone else later, I'll be more knowledgeable about working at that company. Also, I feel a lot more comfortable when I'm in charge of the conversation flow. I usually leave information interviews more positive about the opportunities at the company and feel more confident about the way my first appearance to the company went over. With a traditional interview, I make sure that I'm prepared with background information on the company and pertinent questions that I want to ask. I also make sure to review what my answers will be to the most commonly asked interview questions. I have a few books and information packets that have been helpful, not only with preparing for interviews but throughout the entire job-hunting process.

COVER LETTERS

You improve your chances of a response by writing a brief cover letter to accompany your résumé. Not only is it common courtesy to introduce yourself, but you make life a little easier for the company representative by mentioning the position that interests you. And it wouldn't hurt to take enough time to learn something about the company (start with their Web sites), and mention specifically why you would be a good fit for the job. (See examples in this chapter.)

CHECKING WHAT THE EMPLOYER WILL SEE

Before sending off your résumé for real, e-mail it and your cover letter to yourself. This way you can fix all the glitches and not risk rejection from an employer before you get a chance to discuss the job itself.

SAMPLE RÉSUMÉS

The first two of the following résumés were designed for use in job interviews. The last four were electronically generated and downloaded. You may find specific wording and phraseology in one or more of them that will help you construct and design your own résumés. The four electronic résumés are accompanied by cover letters intended to introduce the writers' backgrounds and interests. Visually these four résumés are identical to the first two. More frequently, though, electronically generated résumés will look like just another e-mail message and appear in a "typewriter" typeface (called "Courier").

Business Analyst (Entry Level)

Kelly A. Irish

Current Address	**Permanent Address**
Boston College	4350 39th Place North
Ignacio Hall B51 Box 9171	Plymouth, MN 55446
Chestnut Hill, MA 02467	(612) 555-1066
(617) 555-8152	irishk@bc.edu

OBJECTIVE
   Dynamic position where my leadership, business, and interpersonal skills will be utilized and developed.

EDUCATION
Boston College   Chestnut Hill, MA
   Wallace E. Carroll School of Management
   B.S. in Information Systems, May 2001
   Cumulative GPA: 3.3/4.0 Dean's List

WORK EXPERIENCE
Boston College Finance Department   Chestnut Hill, MA
   October 1999–Present
   Developed Finance faculty members' personal Web pages. Trained professors to maintain and update pages.

Cargill, Inc.   Minneapolis, MN
   Electronic Commerce Intern—Summer 2000
   Researched suppliers, customers, and online marketplaces to support Cargill's e-business strategy. Interviewed present and past interns to assess the internship program, and developed suggestions for improvement. Held two project-related presentations for executives and managers. Interviewed managers to develop an understanding of Cargill businesses. Created a department PowerPoint template. Documented Cargill Business Units Internet sites. Participated in a personality profile system evaluation.

   Internet Group Intern—Summer 1999
   Developed new Web site for Electronic Commerce Gateway group. Researched business partners' needs and developed improved EC service plan. Researched vendor-managed inventory technology and corporate implementation. Developed new employee welcome packet. Coordinated corporate EC meeting.

Kelly A. Irish, pg 2

Service and Strategy Intern—Summer 1998
Researched cellular options for individuals and found appropriate plans for users. Developed and compiled benchmark cellular survey from other companies from which improvements to Cargill's cellular program were implemented. Administrator of Web-based On Line Organizational and Management Directory. Advised with user-side improvements on the rollout of a new chargeback billing system. Coordinated and represented the telecommunications group at the Corporate IT Fair.

Training—December 1997–January 1998
Trained on the new chargeback billing system for future rollout. Converted manual information into system. Verified data links accuracy. Made improvements to user interface.

Receptionist and Secretary—Summer 1997
Drafted letters, sent telexes, prepared purchase orders and shipping requests, maintained supply room and other data entry tasks.

SKILLS
Computer Skills: MS Office Suite, Lotus Suite 3.0, Access, C Programming, MacroMedia Fireworks, Flash, Visual BASIC, HotMetal Pro, Paint Shop Pro, HTML, File Maker Pro
Language Skills: 3 years high school Spanish

ACTIVITIES
4 Boston Volunteer organization: Taught a computer and GED course to multinational low-income adults.
Careers in Management: Boston College students' career preparation and planning organization.
Boston College Ski Club member
Golf and basketball captain at Orono High School and continued enthusiast.

IT Consultant

Paul R. Sagdahl
320 210th Court SE
Sammamish, WA 98053
(425) 555-5590, (206) 555-4527   psagdahl@msn.com

Experience
IBM Global Services, Western Area 11   1997–1999
IT Consulting and Implementation Services
Seattle, WA

Senior Consultant—Currently a Senior Consultant / Contractor specializing in data center relocations, project management, IT infrastructure process redesign, systems availability, and systems management to meet a wide variety of client requirements. Skills include IT management consulting, availability planning, and project management to build IT infrastructures for both legacy systems and client/server information systems.

Accomplishments:
- Facilitated a complex data center relocation team as the Senior Relocation Consultant. Developed their strategic plan. Trained the IBM / client team on the logic of successful relocation planning, published results.
- Conducted a data center physical space redesign for an Alaskan utility downsizing from their S/390 to AS/400. Provided a recommendations guide, a phased AutoCad space plan, and a detailed Project 98 project plan.
- Directed software and tech support portions of a data center consolidation study for a large utility being merged in Houston, Texas.
- Comanaged the Relocation Mission Control Center for a very successful mainframe data center move of a large transportation company from San Francisco to Jacksonville, FL. Also contributed significantly to the Project 98 project plan as the MVS technical consultant and to the data center as the IBM technical lead.
- Recently led a process design reengineering engagement for a large Northwest retail and food store chain. Provided "best practice" IT processes for both the IT management system and manage availability processes to bring them up to state of the art. Provided an outage analysis for insight into solution areas and a detailed process guide with initiatives required for continuous improvement.

US Marketing and Services, Western Area 11   1992–1997
Availability and Operational Services
Seattle, WA

Certified I/S Availability Manager —
Accomplishments:
- Led an engagement for a large Northwest insurance company in identifying 24 x 7 availability requirements. Employed an outage analysis and a trend analysis to quan-

tify exposure areas and recommended technology and process improvements to move toward a solution for their widened up-time goal. Client implemented a number of these recommendations and realized a significant shrinkage of its batch window.
- Over a 4-year period led a multistate insurance company in improving its data center infrastructure to exceed their 99.7 percent "prime time availability to the end user" goal. Then brought outage analysis, root cause analysis, and statistical analysis to this satisfied client on a quarterly basis for an additional year. Due to the value of the "base" recommendations, this advice has been implemented in full.
- Consulted for a large Northwest freight forwarding company on change management processes. The team reviewed changes from the network, project managers, systems software, application software, operations, both online and batch. Recommended process changes to many aspects of change management, as well as the network and production support help desks. This allowed the client to put together a comprehensive solution to its change management discipline.
- Trained by IBM's Project Management Boot Camp, had managed a project to install a high-availability RS/6000 system, a Magstar tape library with new operating system, and applications software components such as ADSM and Systems View. This project was completed on time and on budget with a very high level of customer satisfaction despite a number of early life cycle product issues. This system is now successfully running a university in Seattle.
- Managed an in-house review of management processes within IBM's Pacific Northwest Availability Center. Effective in securing the consensus and detail required to put a 10-binder set of office disciplines process together. Personal focus was on the market management, availability management, and systems assurance disciplines. This internal certification review was a success with three best processes.

Marketing and Services, Bay Trading Area
Bank of America Team 1989–1992
Walnut Creek, CA

Enterprise SE Manager/Consulting Systems Engineer —

Accomplishments:
- Responsible for Bank of America host availability and managing Systems Engineers in San Francisco, Los Angeles, and Concord data centers. This required not only managerial skills, but technical knowledge of MVS, IMS, VM, and TPF operating system environments.
- Helped design and implement high-availability IMS / XRF banking system with 45-second mean-time-to-recovery in the event of mainframe failure.
- Assisted with an availability study that focused on availability process improvements.
- Led the very successful BofA Application Development Data Center move from San Francisco to Concord.

Paul R. Sagdahl, pg 3

Previous Positions

1987–1989	Large Systems Advisory Market Support Rep US Marketing and Services Northwestern Area 11 Staff San Francisco, CA	1983–1985	Technical Assistance Manager National Service Division Northwestern Area Staff San Francisco, CA
1985–1987	Advisory Systems Engineer South West Marketing Division San Francisco Finance San Francisco, CA	1980–1983	Program Support Field Manager National Service Division San Francisco Golden Gate San Francisco, CA

Education and Background

- Executive MBA with an emphasis in organizational behavior—Saint Mary's College
- BA in Management—Saint Mary's, graduating with honors
- ABA in Electronics from Olympic College
- Completed over 3000 hours of technical and professional study within IBM, including e-Business Application Development, NT Server 4.0, CICS Access to the Internet, S/390 Parallel Sysplex Planning, Professional Consulting Workshop, I&TM Methodology, System Management Framework Design, OS/390, Project Management Bootcamp, MVS, VTAM, VM, TSO.

Awards / Certifications

Recertified Availability Manager	1997	Seattle, WA
IBM Golden Circle	1995	San Diego, CA
IBM Services Excellence Award	1994	Seattle, WA
Certified Availability Manager	1994	Dallas, TX
IBM Hundred Percent Club	1989	Orlando, FL
IBM Systems Engineering Symposium	1986	San Francisco, CA
Area Manager's Award	1986	San Francisco, CA

IT Consultant

Gordon Cummings
220 Willis St.
Winnipeg, Manitoba, Canada
S3A 1J3
506-555-9626
gordo@bits.mn.ca

RELOCATION: USA (North Atlantic/New England), Canada—East

OBJECTIVE:
To obtain a position as a network administrator/computer technician that will allow me to apply my existing skills and provide me with an opportunity for continued professional development in the applied field.

QUALIFICATIONS:
Solid communication and interpersonal skills
A well-organized self-starter, effective working both independently and as an integral member of a team effort
Effective working under pressure and within time constraints
Meticulous and detail-oriented resulting in high performance standards
Able to assess situational needs and to implement creative solutions
Dedicated and conscientious, ability to simultaneously manage multiple tasks

CERTIFICATIONS:
MCP Microsoft Certified Professional (Windows 2000 Server)
MCP Microsoft Certified Professional (NT Server 4.0)
CNA Certified Novell Administrator (NetWare 4.11)
A+ Certified (computer repair and upgrade)

EXPERIENCE IN USE OF:
Windows NT Server 4.0
Windows 2000 Server
Windows 2000 Professional
Windows NT Workstation
Windows 9X
Windows NT SBS (Small Business Server) 4.5
Microsoft BackOffice Products (Proxy Server, Exchange Server, IIS)
Windows NT Terminal Server 4.0 (Thin Client)
Windows VPN
Novell NetWare 4.11

Novell Client
MS Office Suite
Corel Office Suite
IE5 and Components
FTP Clients and Server
Various backup software (Arcserv, Backup Exec, NT Backup)
Various antivirus software (Inoculan, Norton, Macafee)
Terminal emulation software (Control IT, PC Anywhere)
RPM remote printing software

EMPLOYMENT:
1998–Present: Bits Consultants, Inc.
Position: Network Consultant/Computer Technician

Provide network consulting services for several small-to-medium-size companies, as well as computer sales and service.

June 1995–Dec. 1995, June 1996–Dec. 1996 (Contract): Province of Manitoba
Department of Fisheries and Aquaculture
Position: Aquaculture Technician

PROFESSIONAL:
Experience: installation, troubleshooting, and administration of servers, workstations (to the board level), printers, modems, and UTP CAT5 cabling.

Installation, troubleshooting, and administration of Network Operating Systems to include NT 4.0 server, NT SBS (Small Business Server) 4.5, NT workstation and NT Terminal Server, Win 9x, Windows 2000, NetWare 4.11 server and client, VPN setup and administration.

Installation, troubleshooting, and administration Microsoft BackOffice products to include Internet Information Server 4.0, Exchange 5.5, and MS Proxy server.

Configuration of LAN using TCP/IP, IPX/SPX, NWLink, NetBEUI, DHCP, DNS, WINS, etc. primarily on NT 4.0 LAN systems with some implementation of Novell NetWare 4.11.

Served as liaison with customers and clients, providing technical support, end user training, and problem resolution for various software applications via phone support and on-site visits.

EDUCATION:
Manitoba West High School—Graduated June 1991

MARKETING BRAND YOU: WHAT TO DO WITH YOUR TARGETED RÉSUMÉ

Gordon Cummings, pg 3

NBCC St. Andrews—Graduated June 1995
Aquaculture Technician Program

1997–98—Job Oriented Training (JOT)
Computer Network Technician/System Support Specialists

INTERESTS & ACTIVITIES:
Scuba diving
Golf
Softball
Fishing

COVER LETTER

Attention Human Resources:

I am interested in expanding my professional experience by seeking new challenges in the area of Information Technology. I am interested in a position with your organization and have enclosed my résumé for review and consideration.

As outlined in the enclosed résumé, I am currently employed as a Network Consultant/Computer Technician, and work closely each day with end users in a variety of environments. I am reliable, trustworthy, and eager to learn. I interact well with people and enjoy working as part of a team as well as independently.

Over the past 2 years I have been exposed to a wide array of network environments and have developed a broad range of knowledge in the applied field. I have also achieved certifications with Microsoft and Novell and am currently working toward MCSE status for Windows 2000.

I feel that with my experience and skills I would be a valuable asset to your organization.

I thank you for your time and look forward to a possible interview.

Sincerely,

Gordon Cummings

Technical Administrator

Antoinette Ridley
17 Morris Road, Whippany, NJ USA 07701
e-mail: aridley112z@aol.com
(201) 555-5050

PROFESSIONAL DEVELOPMENT

April 2000–July 2000
Merrill Lynch, Benefits & Investments Solutions,
Technology Management Group—Chester, NJ

Change Manager
Responsible for receiving, reviewing, and approving emergency or scheduled changes via Microsoft Outlook. Created and maintained daily and monthly reports regarding Mainframe emergency/scheduled changes. Determined the types of emergencies associated with the Mainframe. Created and supported project plans.

May 1999–April 2000
Intel, Inc.
Software Development—Morristown, NJ

Project Administrator
Assisted project leaders/managers in the administration of creating, managing, and maintaining project plans. Responsibilities included: scheduled and resourced data into NaviSys project control system; analyzed scheduling; developed, coordinated, and issued NaviSys roll-up reports; produced project reviews for NaviSys senior management and NaviSys clients; provided Project Workbench training to the project leaders/managers.

April 1998–May 1999
Merrill Lynch, Group Employee Services
Participant Services—Chester, NJ

Project Analyst
Assisted in the development and maintenance of the Knowledge Retrieval System and the Service Request Tracking system. Prepared daily reports for senior management and project managers. Trained employees on data entry for the Knowledge Retrieval System.

October 1995–April 1998
Merrill Lynch, Group Employee Services
Participant Services—Chester, NJ

Antoinette Ridley, pg 2

Administrative Assistant for Section Managers
Scheduling, travel/hotel arrangements, compiling week/month/quarter end reports, inventory control.

August 1994–October 1995
S. Fryczynski & Son, Inc.—Bayonne, NJ

Secretary
Word processing, billing, customer service, scheduling meetings, placing orders and advertisements.

August 1992–April 1994
Edison Savings & Loan—Teaneck, NJ

Bank Teller
Check cashing, updating bankbooks, and recibcukubgbalances.

EDUCATION

May 1999 (2 weeks—Beacon University, Intel Training), Morristown, NJ
Life CAD/MP 3.5 & 4.0, Microsoft Project Workbench, overview of Life Insurance and Annuities pertaining to Intel Software Development.

May 1994—Zoeb Institute, Morristown, NJ
Computer Training Microsoft Office

REFERENCES: Furnished upon request

COVER LETTER
Dear Sir or Madam:

I am actively seeking an opportunity in a demanding, fast-paced multitasking office. My years of experience at Merrill Lynch have equipped me with a multitude of skills, and I would like to continue my growth in your firm.

Throughout my career I have demonstrated for my employers an exceptional ability for meeting organizational objectives and demands. In addition to my technical skills, I am an adept individual. I am certain I would prove to be an asset to your firm.

If my abilities meet the needs of your firm, I would greatly appreciate the opportunity to speak with you personally at your earliest convenience. Thank you for your time.

Sincerely,

Antoinette Ridley

Software Sales

ALEX P. KORSAKOFF
131 Wallace Ave., Apt. #14
Cambridge, MA 02431
Tel: (617) 555-0000
e-mail: korsy@earthlink.net

SALES PROFESSIONAL

Proven top performer with a track record of consistent success.

Adept in all stages of the sales cycle. Strengths in converting opportunities into tangible business, building long-term client relationships, high-level negotiations, and closing the sale.

Highly effective in innovating solutions/strategies to overcome complex problems, achieving positive sales results for both clients and company in record time.

Solid business acumen combined with a consultative sales approach and technical aptitude. Strong interest in selling technology solutions; extensive business-to-business experience includes high tech.

Trilingual: English, Spanish (conversational), and Hebrew. U.S. citizen.

SELECTED ACCOMPLISHMENTS

- Built annual sales from zero base to $15M USD at R.E.O. Personally developed and produced $7–$9M USD in annual sales. Credited by clients for talent in devising creative marketing solutions and negotiating complex deals that resulted in higher sales in significantly less time.
- Delivered $5–$7M USD in annual sales and led sales team to generate $13M USD annually territorywide as Zone Sales Manager.
- Ranked among top 10 for 2 consecutive years out of 300 sales professionals companywide during tenure at a real estate brokerage company. Selected for promotion to commercial Sales Manager in recognition of performance results.
- Initiated and developed new revenue stream that did not previously exist, producing substantial business by cultivating relationships with other brokerage firms.
- Drove sales 300% while raising profit per unit by 25%, turned around nonperforming department, and significantly increased local advertising revenues. Named Sales Manager of the Year out of 30 managers companywide.
- Grew annual import sales from start-up to $1.5M USD and secured exclusive contracts with top exporters at Chana Kristol Management.

PROFESSIONAL EXPERIENCE

Manager—R.E.O. Real Estate Co.
Tel Aviv, Israel, 1997–2000

Founded, established, and managed a profitable commercial real estate business serving investors and mid-to-large high-tech and industrial companies throughout Tel Aviv market. Developed and managed client accounts, creating and executing sales/marketing strategies for commercial projects. Negotiated and closed deals up to $8M USD. Worked closely/negotiated with corporate executives, investors, accountants, attorneys, mortgage brokers, architects, advertising, and other professional services. Recruited, trained, motivated, and supervised sales and administrative staff.

Zone Sales Manager—Dennis Barak Real Estate and Investments, Ltd.
Tel Aviv, Israel, 1994–1997

Managed sales and marketing activities for all commercial projects in a $20M USD territory encompassing three city zones of $2B USD real estate brokerage company with 60 offices nationwide. Developed and managed client base comprising industrial and high-tech companies, working with senior-level executives. Negotiated and closed deals up to $5M USD. Managed sales force and created exclusive territories for each person, improving productivity and enhancing teamwork. Structured and implemented sales quotas, advertising, and incentive programs that contributed to performance improvement.

Sales Manager—InterNadlan, Ltd.
Tel Aviv, Israel, 1991–1994

Provided strategic management direction to the advertising sales and day-to-day operations of a zone newspaper at the largest newspaper publishing company nationwide. Diverse scope of responsibilities included budgeting, sales, marketing as well as oversight of advertising layout, graphics, printing, and other related activities. Designed and executed a series of innovative strategies that reversed declining sales trend and resulted in a 300% increase in advertising sales; newspaper more than doubled from 40 to 96 pages. Recruited, developed, and supervised sales, computer graphics, marketing, and support staff. Negotiated with customers, suppliers, and municipalities.

Import Manager—Chana Kristol Management
Beer Sheva, Israel, 1988–1991

Recruited while attending the university to establish and manage import operations of a midsize industrial company with 100 employees. Reported to the CEO and represented company at international trade shows throughout Europe. Negotiated sole agent

Alex P. Korsakoff, pg 3

contracts with key export companies and managed all activities from securing financing (letters of credit) to delivery and customs. Supervised department staff.

EDUCATION

Master's in Information Technology, 1998
Harvard University, Cambridge, Massachusetts

M.S., Industry and Management Engineering, 1992
Ben Gurion University, Beer Sheva, Israel

B.S., with honors, Psychology, 1984
Michigan State University, East Lansing, Michigan
Phi Kappa Phi Honors

COVER LETTER

Dear Sir/Madam,
If you are conducting a search for a sales professional who can deliver sales volume and profit objectives through expertise in strategic sales/marketing planning, long-term relationship building, and high-level negotiations, my background may interest you.

My success in sales is based on several factors:
- Creative planning and going the extra mile to achieve results.
- Skill in managing a territory, qualifying leads, negotiating, and moving them to closure.
- Selling solutions to customer problems and supporting sales with superior service.
- Business savvy and persuasive communication skills.

This strategy has served me well, and I would welcome the opportunity to put it to work as a member of your sales team. A results-oriented self-starter and focused professional, I am interested in transferring my sales/marketing skills to the high-tech/e-commerce industry. To complement my sales experience, I am pursuing an IT degree on a part-time basis.

I am confident in my ability to make a substantial contribution that will translate into increased sales for your company. As my clients will confirm, I have a knack for innovating solutions to major challenges and closing deals that result in higher sales in record time.

If one of your client companies is searching for a sales representative who is customer driven with proven business development, sales, and marketing talent, then I would welcome a conversation. Thank you for your consideration.

Sincerely,

Alex P. Korsakoff

Computer Programmer

William Lowell
13915 Jefferson Street
Montpelier, VT 05301
802-555-8614 (Home)
low@uvm.edu

OBJECTIVE
To obtain a job in software development or related computer science / IT field

CAREER SUMMARY

Strong technical aptitude
- Excellent customer service skills
- Developed C/C++, Object Oriented programming skills
- Strong communications skills
- LAN administration
- Proven ability to work well with different departments and personnel within a company

TECHNICAL SKILLS

- C/C++ (MS Visual C++)
- Visual Basic
- Object Oriented Programming
- HTML
- UNIX
- DOS
- Novell Netware
- Windows NT / NT Server
- MS Office Suite

WORK EXPERIENCE

IBM
Summer Hire, May 2000–August 2000

- Worked with database management creating new databases and upgrading using Microsoft Access and Microsoft Excel. Extensive use of macros and Visual Basic programming.
- Perform complex calculations as part of an engineering team
- User support for the LAN using Windows, NT, NT Server, and Exchange Server

Addison County Health Care System
Y2K Assistance Team, June 1999–July 1999

- Perform Year 2000 testing, inventory tracking, and remediation for desktop networks at four hospitals in the North County HCA Health System: St. Albans Medical Center, Northwestern Medical Center, Fletcher Allen Hospital, and Yankee Medical Inc.
- Created Y2K remediation program in C++, which reduced overall remediation time

PC/LAN Administrator, July 1999–August 1999
- Network administration
- New user setup
- Performed troubleshooting tasks
- Development of Access Databases using Visual Basic

EDUCATION

University of Vermont, Burlington, VT
- Bachelor of Science–May 2001
- Major: Mathematics–Applied Discrete Option (CS Heavy)
- Minor: Computer Science

Honors:
- Deans List

COVER LETTER

Dear Sir or Madam:

I am a recent graduate from the University of Vermont. I graduated with a B.S. in Mathematics and a minor in Computer Science. I am looking to find a career in computer programming using C/C++. I am looking for a career in the New England area. I have a strong background in Object Oriented design and programming. I have an excellent understanding of Networks, TCP/IP, and COM/DCOM, which I have used in some of my programming cousework. I have taken six semesters of programming courses while at the University of Vermont, with a GPA of 2.96.

I have been a member of the Vermont volleyball team for 4 years and have a excellent understanding of what it takes to be a team player. I have had experience working as part of a large team while at a large engineering division of IBM, where I worked on a team to aid in design of a railroad system.

Thank you for your time, and I look forward to hearing from you. If you have any questions, please contact me by either e-mail or phone.

Respectfully yours,
William Lowell

MARKETING BRAND YOU

There are several routes you can take now that your electronic and hard-copy paperwork is ready to go:

- Contacting target companies
- Contacting recruitment firms and job sites
- Contacting online job-search portals
- Networking and information interviewing

Direct Contact with Targeted Companies

If you are positioned, ready to move, and know what companies you want most to work for, learn as much as you can about each of them. If you know the names of the companies that interest you, start with their Web sites. This will give you relatively thorough information about goods and services, corporate culture, mission, and key officers. But because the Web site serves largely as an online brochure, it presents the company's best face. You'll have to look elsewhere for the warts. Here are a few good sources:

- *Hoover's Online (www.hoovers.com).* Hoover's Online is a premier online information resource for businesspeople, offering free, advertising-supported information, as well as in-depth data available through basic or enterprisewide business subscriptions. Its 3 million users include corporate executives, sales and marketing professionals, recruiters, business development managers, and job seekers. At the core of Hoover's Online is a database of company coverage on some 65,000 public and private enterprises worldwide and the industries in which they operate. (Hoover's offers 30 days of free access to any student with an .edu e-mail address. Individual subscriptions are available for $29.95 per month and $199.95 per year.)

- *bizjournals.com (www.bizjournals.com).* If you are relocating and are sure of your destination, you can get a jump on business information in your new hometown (provided it's 1 of the 40 largest U.S. cities) with a 1-year subscription to that city's weekly publication, dedicated to the most complete, up-to-date business news. Annual subscriptions range from $52 (Birmingham) to $86 (Kansas City).
- *CompaniesOnline (www.companiesonline.com).* For a list of target companies hiring people in your specialty, along with all basic information, here is a good source. Click Computers and Software, which includes 10 categories (e.g., Data Processing, Information Storage and Retrieval, Maintenance and Repair, Programming Services, System Integration). Pick your favorite—let's say Computer Data Processing, which on one particular day led to the identification of 4851 companies. The downside is that they are randomly entered and neither alphabetized nor classified by state. So if you are interested in just one or two locations, it could be a time-consuming search.

As you compile research about your target companies, look carefully for information about new developments—acquisitions, product lines, or reorganization specifics, for example—that may be useful to write an effective cover letter to accompany your résumé or to fortify your interviews with company executives.

Recruitment Firms and Job Sites

Dozens of Internet sites specialize in job search, recruitment, career change, and vocational counseling. Some maintain relationships with the corporate world and are clearinghouses for résumés sent in application for open positions. Following are Internet addresses for some of them in all four categories. Familiarize yourself with as many sites as are manage-

MARKETING BRAND YOU: WHAT TO DO WITH YOUR TARGETED RÉSUMÉ

able for you and register with all of those that provide the kinds of information and services that meet your specific needs.

www.hotjobs.com
www.6figurejobs.com
http://jobs.internet.com
www.theworksite.com
www.wetfeet.com
www.monster.com
www.flipdog.com

www.kforce.com
www.careermosaic.com
www.vault.com
www.headhunter.com
www.craiglist.com
www.jobsonline.com
www.careerbuilder.com

Advice from the Pros

Despite recent cutbacks in recruiting departments, job seekers still turn to executive recruiters in their searches. Here are five tips on working with recruiters, from the Cleveland-based Management Recruiters International (www.mri.com):

1. *Be professional.* Work with a recruiter as if that person were your colleague, your manager, or your client.
2. *Be honest.* Explain the extent of your job-search efforts and results. Don't conceal anything from the recruiter.
3. *Be forthright.* Explicitly share with your recruiter what you are, or are not, willing to do for your next job, especially regarding salary or relocation. Don't hesitate to give feedback after interviews are completed to let the recruiter know if you are still interested in the job.
4. *Be committed.* Follow up on what you promise to do. A lack of commitment will discourage recruiters from working with you.
5. *Be proactive.* Research recruiters in your industry even before you start actively looking for a job. That way, you'll already have the contacts you need when you want to begin a job search.

www.dice.com www.nettemps.com
www.brassring.com www.jobtrack.com

Career-Oriented Portals and Search Engines

Start with the major search engines if you have not yet narrowed in on a list of companies that are of paramount interest to you: Google, Yahoo, Excite@Home, HotBot, Infoseek, AltaVista, Lycos, and LookSmart, and any others that may be in operation by the time you read this. Each offers job-search services of varying kinds and quality. Most of these portals also catalog URLs offering career assistance and advice, résumé posting and marketing services, city and state resource centers, employment ads in publications, executive recruiters, and a variety of job databases worldwide. One of the more comprehensive of these portals is Yahoo. Let's walk through the options at this site to see what we might learn:

- On Yahoo's home page (www.yahoo.com) click Employment and Work under the heading Business and Economy.
- This leads to the option of choosing the general category Yahoo Careers or any one of 20-odd specialized categories (Career Planning, Recruiting and Placement, Salary Information, U.S. State Government Agencies, etc.). Let's click the general option Yahoo Careers.
- The Yahoo Careers page includes another half dozen major options (Find a Job, Salaries & Benefits, Career Growth, and Recruit among them). Let's try Find a Job.
- Here you can pick a major U.S. city and browse through the jobs available from current classified ads.
- On any city page you select are a number of additional possibilities: For example, five Research Tools (Salaries, Companies, Industries, Occupations, and Relocation); a Browse Jobs option (numerous IT positions under the subcategories Engineering,

Information Technology, and Media, Arts, and Design); and profiles of leading companies headquartered in that city. Under any of these categories is a rich cache of information. The Companies option under Research Tools, for example, features in-depth company profiles of more than 1000 companies (through a link to www.WetFeet.com). Relocation, a little farther down, allows you to compare U.S. cities by cost of living, real estate, and quality of life, among other things. HomeFair (www.homefair.com) offers a similar service.

Networking and Information Interviewing

More people—by an overwhelming factor—are hired through networking than in any other way. Put simply, networking improves your chances of finding a job in direct proportion to the number of people you meet in your function, specialty, and industry. Be shameless. Use your family, your friends, your colleagues, your school, church, and community acquaintances to get the word out. Attend trade fairs and conventions in your field. Keep a supply of business cards and résumés available at all times. Master a 30-second description of your background and accomplishments that you are able transmit to anyone in a position to help you. From the employer's point of view, finding a good person cost-free is an attractive alternative. Saving the price of recruitment fees, advertising, and human resources department hours—all allocated to the hiring process—gives qualified candidates an added advantage (albeit slight!) in the eyes of the hiring authority. You've heard of the hidden job market? This is the rock you'll find it under.

Information interviews, similarly, offer the opportunity to interact with decision makers in your function or specialty. Networking, in fact, is an ideal forum for generating information interviews with individuals willing to describe the inner workings of a company that interests you or to provide an advantages-disadvantages ratio for a slight change of career you've been considering.

To set up an information interview, don't even suggest that you're looking for a job—just information. And this should be the truth. Make your meeting an information *exchange*, offering what you know about situations your interviewer may ask you about. Prepare your questions in advance and follow up each interview with a brief letter of appreciation. You've just added a valuable networking contact. He or she has helped you. Maybe you can return the favor down the road.

CHAPTER ELEVEN

Avoiding Interview Potholes

What you should know first is that the job doesn't always go to the best-qualified candidate. There are exceptions—most of them are job seekers lucky enough to interview at companies that screen out candidates long on personality but short on fitness for the job. If you're applying at a dot-com start-up, the hiring process likely will not be that rigorous. A fully functioning human resources department, after all, is not one of a new company's first priorities. There are many other more important situations to address, so interviewing usually is done on the fly. If some of the advice offered throughout the rest of this chapter sounds "pushy" to you, it's because we're assuming that interviewing is not your interviewer's day job. This means that you will be doing much of the work, including matching your qualifications to the job's requirements and conveying your suitability for the job to your interviewer. When you interview in a more civilized work environment, just scale back your involvement accordingly. But enough cynicism. Here are the keys to a successful interview, regardless of how effective your interviewer is.

PRELIMINARY TELEPHONE INTERVIEWS

Frequently a company will screen marginal candidates to assure that only the most qualified are brought in for face-to-face interviews. The most convenient way to do this—for interviewee as well as interviewer—is to spend time on the phone to be certain that a potentially good applicant is not overlooked.

If you are asked to talk by phone with a company representative, everything you read throughout the rest of this chapter is applicable. The difference is that you won't get to present your qualifications in anywhere as leisurely a fashion as you would in an on-site interview. Your single objective is to make a positive enough impression during your phone interview to upgrade your candidacy to the next level. In addition to taking time to research the company, here are the four steps crucial to generating an in-person interview:

1. Ask for a specific definition of the ideal candidate.
2. Project yourself as that candidate.
3. Find out which two or three problems must be solved first.
4. Demonstrate your ability and willingness to solve them.

PREPARING FOR RÉSUMÉ-RELATED QUESTIONS

Actually, your job begins a step earlier, with your ability to apply only for those jobs that interest you and for which you are qualified. You can save a lot of wheel spinning by separating fact from fantasy in the job search. Be honest enough with yourself to distinguish between a job that would be great to have from a job you are competent enough to do well. You'll reach this conclusion all by yourself, presumably, after getting hit on the head with enough rejection letters—or worse, no response at all to your résumé and cover letter submissions. But save yourself that month or two of walking in place. Match your skills and accomplishments with the requirements for any given job. Go for it only if the prospective match realistically exists.

Before the interview, go over the résumé the interviewer has (if you have prepared more than one version) and treat every entry almost as a script cue. You were brought in for the interview because some of your assignments and accomplishments were of interest. If you have been able to find out specifically why you are being interviewed, you'll be that much further ahead. If not, go over your résumé line for line and try to anticipate which of your qualities are most likely to have generated the company's interest in you. Think of responses to questions that will allow you to elaborate on your accomplishments.

On a sheet of paper, make two columns. Keeping in mind the requirements for the job and what you believe the company is looking for, use your résumé to prepare discussing your accomplishments. In the left-hand column, list those accomplishments. In the right-hand column, explain why and how you attained them.

PREPARING FOR TOUGH QUESTIONS

Every experienced interviewer asks one or more tough questions. Some interviewers seem to ask nothing *but* tough questions. Basically, they just want to know what you can offer their company, why you want to leave (or have left) your present position, and what your strengths and weaknesses are.

The best way to handle such questions is to anticipate them and be prepared for them. Write all your answers to the following questions on a sheet of paper, then memorize and practice them so that when the questions are asked, you'll be ready.

- What do you know about our company? (Do the research so you'll have some key information.)

- Why do you want to work for us? (Things to think about in formulating your answer: challenge, growth potential, experience in the field.)
- What would you do for us? What can you do for us that someone else can't? (Make sure your answer relates to the company's needs.)
- What about this position do you find the most attractive? The least attractive? (Careful!)
- Why should we hire you? (Not because you need a job. Think about specific contributions you can make.)
- Do you object to taking a drug-screening test? (Make sure you know exactly where you stand on this one, what you are willing to do, and what you're not. An increasing number of firms are requiring drug screening as part of their preemployment physical.)
- You may be overqualified for the position we have to offer. (Think about how your experience is an asset and what kind of potential there is in the position for the person who may be more "qualified.")
- Are you a good manager? (Prepare several examples.)
- What do you see as the most difficult task in being a manager or executive?
- Why do you want to leave your present job? (Don't lie if you've recently been fired, but do put the best face on it. Don't be complaining, accusatory, or negative about your previous firm. Think about "differences in approach.")

Question to Candidate

"One question I always end up asking is: 'If I were to go out on the street and talk to your peers, your ex-colleagues, and your customers, what would they say about you?' I go through this list one group at a time and invariably get useful and interesting answers."

—Paul Rand, President
Corporate Technology Communications

- Where do you want to be in 5 years? (Relate your long-term goals to those of the company you're interviewing with.)
- How many people did you supervise on your last job? (Indicate any supervisory growth from a previous position, if applicable.)
- What do your subordinates think of you? (Positive specifics are relevant.)
- What are the five most significant accomplishments in your career so far? In your last position?
- If I spoke with your previous bosses, what would they say are your greatest strengths and weaknesses? (Think about acceptable weaknesses in terms of requirements for the job.)
- Do you prefer staff or line work? Why?
- In your present position, what problems have you identified that had previously been overlooked?
- If you had your choice of jobs and companies, where would you go? (You do have your choice, and the interviewer's company is it.)
- Tell me about yourself. (Talk about specific job-related accomplishments that demonstrate skills you think will meet the company's needs.)
- What are your strong points?
- What are your weak points? (No one is perfect. The trick is to find an acceptable weakness in terms of the job for which you are applying, then talk about what you've done to improve it.)
- If you could start again, what would you do differently? (Of course there are things you would do differently, but don't blame others for your misfortune.)
- What are your goals? What have you done to reach them?

PREPARING FOR HIDDEN AGENDA QUESTIONS

The first cousin to the tough question is the hidden agenda question. When there is a question behind the question, the interviewer is attempting to find out one thing by asking another. You need to recognize just what the interviewer is getting at—and then provide a well-thought-out answer.

- How would you evaluate your last employer? (*Are you a complainer? Do you take responsibility for your actions? Are you vindictive or self-pitying?*)
- Who was your best boss? Describe him/her. (*What environment and management style are you most comfortable with?*)
- What are you looking for in a job? (*Does this job match the applicant's needs?*)
- Please give me your definition of the position for which you are being interviewed. (*Does the applicant's idea of the position match the reality in this company?*)
- What is your management philosophy? (*Does your philosophy match the company's?*)
- How long would you stay with us? (*Is this person going to be worth our investment?*)
- In your current or last position, what did you like most? Least? (*How does this fit with the reality of what it's like to work in this company?*)
- As a manager, what do you look for in hiring people? (*Is it the same thing this company looks for?*)

THE FOUR PARTS OF AN INTERVIEW

Breaking any job interview into its component parts is the most effective way both to know what to expect and to prepare accordingly to do your best. There are four parts, or stages, that distinguish most job interviews:

- Make the best first impression.
- Get a definition of the ideal candidate.

> ### Company Recruiters as Interviewers
>
> "Our methodology is a little different from most companies, as I understand it. There are three people on our recruitment team I call Internet geologists. They go through some tough training, but they're able to search strings, to really drill down into Web sites: They'll flip sites, x-ray them all the way down to the personal Web pages. (It's not uncommon for many of the technical people to want to show off a bit and put their résumés on their personal pages.)
>
> "But these aren't the people we're after. The ones with résumés are trolling. We're looking for candidates who aren't looking for us. We just did a swing from our Seattle office and interviewed 12 people for sales positions. The two we liked were the only ones who had *not* posted résumés. When we got to them we asked what their most desirable position would be if they were to make a change. We found out where their horsepower was not being tapped directly and were able to give them what they didn't have."
>
> —K.C. Donovan, Vice President, Human Resources
> *Globix Corporation*

- Determine whether you want the job.
- Work to get either a job offer or a second interview.

Make the Best First Impression

Given two or more candidates with similar credentials, the job will almost invariably go to the individual who projects honesty, sincerity, and enthusiasm. Your appearance, your body language, your attitude—even your vocabulary and diction—all contribute to the first impression you make. This is as important in a preliminary human resources department interview for a larger company as it is with a line manager or company officer. The reason? *Any* company representative can screen you out as easily as screen you in.

> "Whenever two people meet, there are really six people present. There is each man as he sees himself, each man as the other person sees him, and each man as he really is."
>
> —William James

Research the company, the job, and the boss. Your feeling of confidence can singularly affect a first impression, which can be generated initially by something as fundamental as sound preparation. Don't underestimate it. It starts the self-fulfilling prophecy. Your confidence level will lead to an attitude that the company needs you rather than the other way around. Feel successful, and chances are better that you will *be* successful.

Nothing impresses an interviewer like a candidate interested enough to have actually learned something about the company before showing up. Step one is to own the intrinsic skills and experience you know are expected. Step two, being able to apply them to the company you have taken the trouble to research is what will put you over the top. (See Chapter 10 for a list of company research sources.)

Dress appropriately. The dress code at many dot-coms and smaller Internet companies is casual. Three-piece suits are out; chinos and sport shirts are in. (The T-shirt, shorts, and bare feet ensembles definitely exist, but showing up for the first time in such an outfit may be pressing the point.) At larger, more established companies, the uniform of the day is still suit or sport jacket and tie for men, suits or street dresses for women. If you're not sure, hang out near the front door the day before your interview. If you're coming a distance, call someone in human resources before you leave. Also, arrive early enough for a rest room check for lettuce between your teeth, or whatever. The point here is not to make a fashion statement, but to wear or do nothing that detracts from the basic message you are trying to convey: I can do the job, and I will fit in comfortably with my future coworkers.

Maintain a positive attitude; communicate enthusiasm. If you hear something about the job you like, say so. If you can address a need with a tangible accomplishment, recount it. Keep in mind that your interviewer is trying to visualize you in the job. Make that an easy task.

Look for openings in the interview to strengthen your candidacy. Don't wait until the end of the interview to make your own points. Deliver them *in context*. For example, after answering an interviewer's question, ask one of your own on a related point. Questions you have about the job that haven't been covered by the end of the interview can be asked then. ("Do you have any questions?" "Yes, I do.")

Be prepared to discuss a recent termination. If you were fired or laid off at your last job or the one before, this will be difficult to hide, so be prepared to deal with it. Do it honestly, but not defensively. Much less stigma is attached to losing a job today than was the case 15 years or so ago. Spend some time developing answers to the different ways this subject could come up. It will go smoothly if you remember four points:

1. Don't knock your former employer.
2. Don't dwell on negatives.
3. Accept any responsibility you deserve.
4. Identify positive outcomes.

Get a Definition of the Ideal Candidate

The biggest reason for knowing the profile of the ideal candidate—early in the interview—is to enable you to match your qualities against the interviewer's description of that person. Good interviewers not only will allow you to do this but will also make it easy for you. It is in their best interests to hire the best. But in the Internet world, particularly the land of start-up dot-coms, experienced interviewers are not the first to be hired. You may have to assume some of this responsibility yourself. But first you need a thorough understanding of the position. Your goal is not just to get the definition but to be that candidate as honestly as you can. Here's how:

Listen with 100 percent of your concentration. In an interview situation, you can work so hard to frame an answer to the interviewer's question that you lose concentration and miss a crucial, job-related point. It is key to listen with all of your antennae at this important part of the interview. (Asking "What was that again?" in the interview will not necessarily improve your chances.)

Ask questions that illuminate the job. Get specific about aspects of the opening that aren't part of the initial description. Find out if this is a promotable position, what the prospects are for cross training. Other possibilities:

- Who are the people I will be working with?
- What is my immediate supervisor's history in the company?
- Does the company have an orientation program for newly hired employees?
- What training programs does the company offer?
- How do I become familiar with policies and procedures?
- What is the predominant management style at the company?
- What challenges do you think the company will face in the next year? In the next several years?
- What is the culture? What is it like to work here?
- (If a relocation) Where can I get information about housing, cost of living, religious and social organizations, shopping, commuting, schools, recreational facilities, etc.?

Prepare your questions beforehand. Use 3- by 5-inch cards to write out questions you may forget to ask. Check off those you're able to deal with during the course of the interview and ask the others just before you leave. For example, it may be useful for you to know:

- How long has the job been open? (If the answer is 2 months or more, why has it been so difficult to fill?)
- Where is the person who previously held it? (Can you talk to him/her?)
- How many people have been interviewed so far?

> ### Referral Programs Bear Fruit
>
> "The most effective way we have of attracting the best people is our referral program. It was put in place in 1994, the year we started. The research is pretty consistent: In both large companies and small, the most dynamic search engine consists of hiring good people and letting them select new employees *they* know and respect. The existing staff acts as a screening mechanism, and we reward them if the new hires last 3 months. (They usually do.)"
>
> —Gary Alpert, President
> WetFeet.com

- How many candidates are still in the running? (Why are they still being considered?)
- What are the prospects for advancement?
- How is good performance measured?

You may not feel comfortable asking all of these questions—and some of them may not be appropriate to ask your interviewer at the first meeting. If you are working with a recruiter or employment agency, however, this is information they can get for you before you meet your prospective employer face-to-face.

Take notes of information difficult to retain. Don't trust your memory to hold and prioritize facts you may need either in writing a follow-up letter or in conducting further research on the company. As a courtesy, ask, "Do you mind if I take notes?" as you take out your notebook (or use the other side of the 3- by 5-inch cards on which you wrote your interview questions). There is little chance you will be refused.

Communicate your position-related strengths. Take advantage of any opportunity to match your applicable skill sets and accomplishments with the challenges of the open position. Your first chance will come after the job and the ideal candidate have been described. As closely as you can, list your strengths in the sequence offered in the job description given to you by the interviewer.

Determine Whether You Want the Job

There are a few ways for you to find out details about the job, the corporate culture, and the extent to which you fit the position other than by listening to the interviewer.

Verify the company's stability. One obvious piece of information is of particular value to you, especially if you're interviewing with a pre-IPO dot-com company. Conduct enough due diligence to be sure sufficient funding is in place to keep those paychecks coming for the next few months. It's one thing to take a calculated risk for a start-up rich in talent and vision and with a viable market niche (and therefore attractive to venture capitalists). It's quite another to treat the interviewing company as worthy of deep-pocket *Fortune* 100 status without asking enough qualifying questions to validate your assumption.

Find out why the job is available. The best possible answer to this question is that the replaced employee has been promoted, transferred to another division or department as part of a better opportunity, or recruited away by a competitor. If the person was fired or resigned because of incompatibility with another employee (whether boss or peer) still on the payroll, that's a big red flag. You need to probe further to be sure you're not setting yourself up for the same fate.

Find out what you would have to change about yourself to be an effective employee. For example, what is the maximum distance you would be willing to commute? Is there too small a support staff for you to function efficiently? Is the company ripe for a takeover or downsizing? Does the position require too much of a learning curve for you to make an immediate contribution?

Work to Get a Job Offer—or at Least a Second Interview

Neutralize any soft spots in your candidacy. This is the time in the interview when you try to determine if there are any objections to your candidacy.

Let it all hang out because you may never know if you're already blackballed if you don't ask. Here's the question that should do it: "Is there anything I've said that gives you less than total confidence in my ability to do the job?" If you're dealing with an interviewer willing to be honest, you'll find out what you need to do to resurrect your candidacy. It may just be a misunderstanding or an interviewer who hasn't listened intently enough. In any case, this is probably your last opportunity to find out why you won't make the cut—and what you can do about it.

Find out where you stand with the other candidates. It will be useful for you to know whether the interviewing process is just beginning or is in its final stages. You can find out by asking two questions: (1) "What is your timing in coming to a decision to hire?" and (2) "Can you tell me at this point whether I'll be one of those to reach the next round?"

Reaffirm your interest in the job. It doesn't hurt to let the interviewer know you want the job. Restate your qualifications and give it a little enthusiasm.

Elevate your candidacy by any means possible. Tell the interviewer that if it gets down to a close contest between you and another candidate, you'd be willing to take on a trial assignment to demonstrate your ability to do any aspect of the job about which there might be some question or doubt.

You've done all you can. Thank the interviewer for his or her time, and leave. (Don't forget the firm handshake.)

PREPARING FOR THE SECOND INTERVIEW

As one of the finalists for the position you're after, it is important to go into the second interview thoroughly prepared. The competition is stiffer this time around. One way to do this is to get out another two sheets of paper, or easier, set up two three-column tables on your word processor in landscape format. In the first chart, deal with the assets you bring to the opportunity. The left-hand column will list your qualifications for the job; the center column, the extent to which you covered each qualification in the first interview; the third column, the points you yet need to make regarding each qualification. It will look like this:

ASSETS

| My Qualifications | Extent Covered Previously | Points Yet to Be Made |

Set up your liabilities table in similar fashion. Realistically assess your weaknesses in meeting the needs of the job and list the strategies you will use to overcome any objections to your candidacy.

LIABILITIES

| Job Requirements | My Weakness | How I Will Overcome |

As for applying your conclusions to the second interview, you need to strike a proper balance. If you oversell—either in reinforcing positives or eliminating negatives—you risk appearing anxious at one extreme and defensive at the other. Either could knock you out of a job offer. Stay on top of the situation, judging what issues are yet a concern, and then deal with them in a straightforward, confident manner. If an opening occurs, this might be a good time to volunteer a trial assignment for an area where the interviewer perceives you to be weak but for which you have confidence in your ability.

Finally, if things are going well—and this suggestion does involve some risk—consider putting some distance between you and the competition by seizing the day with a forcing question such as "Well, what can I do to convince you that I'm the best person for the job?" or, with a slight smile, "What is preventing you from offering me the job right now?"

But be careful when using this strategy. Depending on your interviewer, this could be a master stroke or a disaster. If you're dealing with an open, pragmatic, forceful individual, you might be viewed as having just the kind of confidence level the company needs. A more reflective, controlled person, however, might well judge such questions to be boorish or otherwise inappropriate. This might be enough to knock you out of the running. Such an individual will require a more subtle approach.

CHAPTER TWELVE

Negotiating Compensation

A survey conducted for CareerPath.com (now a "megajobsearch" site known as CareerBuilder) rated salary as being most important when deciding whether to accept a job offer, according to 89 percent of the respondents. However, more than 50 percent of the workers who completed the survey believe they are underpaid.

And it's true: The way a company compensates its employees tells much about the way it values them. Competitive compensation not only attracts good people, it motivates and helps retain them. For this reason it is in the best interests of both the employee and the employer to reach a mutually satisfactory and equitable compensation agreement.

But compensation is more than base salary. It can include equity or stock; it can include bonuses of various kinds; and it almost always will include benefits. Companies unable to offer competitive starting salaries often can make up the difference with a sign-on bonus or an improved benefits package or performance bonus program.

This is another way of saying that enlightened employers will make it a priority to accommodate the needs of exceptional candidates. Negotiating total compensation, therefore, is almost always an option.

> ## Stock Options: Quickie Definitions
>
> **Stock option:** The right to buy stock at a certain price at a certain time
>
> **Strike price:** The price at which the option holder can buy the stock
>
> **Vesting schedule:** Schedule for receiving options; most commonly spread out over 3 years, with one-third of the options vesting each year
>
> **Exercising options:** Once you have the options, actually buying the stock at the strike price
>
> **Lockup period:** The 6-month period after an initial public offering (IPO) during which company insiders cannot sell their shares
>
> **Alternative minimum tax:** The tax you might be subject to if you have a hefty options package
>
> **"Under water":** The unfortunate condition of having worthless options (i.e., if you have the right to buy stock at $15 and the stock falls to $10, your options are under water)
>
> —iVillage.com

THE EMPLOYMENT CONTRACT

An increasing number of Internet companies are offering employment contracts not just to their officers or executive management team but to all managers and supervisors. In setting up a board of advisors to help formulate a compensation policy for Corporate Technology Communications, Paul Rand went even further. "I included both legal and accounting counsel," says Rand, "and we decided early on that every employee would get a contract. Part of the reason was that we wanted everyone to consciously sign a document that would represent a commitment on both sides—so that they would understand what their responsibilities were, as well as specifically what they would receive for discharging them."

Depending on specific needs and considerations, such a document will include some or all of the following provisions.

- Term or duration of employment
- Description of duties
- Base salary
- Sign-on bonus
- Performance bonuses of various kinds
- Medical, dental, and life insurance
- Relocation expenses where applicable (sometimes to include company purchase and disposition of the old residence and/or company assumption of closing costs of the new residence)
- Low- or no-interest loans
- Equity and/or stock options
- Periodic payment of company-related expenses of various kinds
- Luxury perks, such as limousines or club memberships
- Contingency clauses (often called golden parachutes) in the event of company change of ownership
- Severance conditions (amount, frequency, and duration)
- Contract termination conditions (both for employee and employer)

John Tarrant's *Perks and Parachutes* is the best book available on the subject and contains thorough advice on both contract preparation and negotiation. Sample contracts included vary from simple letters of agreement to a copy of the monster deal signed by Disney's Michael Eisner in 1989.

"Taxes are the number one consideration of employment contracts," says Christopher Loiacono, a CPA, partner, and new-media specialist with New York–based Richard A. Eisner & Company, "and no one focuses on that. If someone says, 'I'm getting options on 100,000 shares. If the stock goes to $30 a share I'll be worth $15 million,' I'll say, 'Wait a

> ### Stock Options Shrink as Layoffs Increase
>
> "The dot-com craze threw conventional practice out the window: Stock options were given to every employee, including many who didn't understand what stock options were, and pretty much any company gave out stock options as a way of hiring talent on the cheap.
>
> "It's not surprising that there have been claims made by employees against dot-coms about stock options. Employees who were promised fabulous wealth for working around the clock in low-paying jobs are now finding themselves out of work because their employers are out of business—or if they're lucky, they have a job but their stock options are essentially worthless. As a result they're angry, disillusioned, and looking to blame someone."
>
> —Nick Crincoli, new-media specialist
Morrison & Foerster (Los Angeles–based law firm)

minute. You'll be worth $7.5 million after you pay taxes on it—and the *remaining* $7.5 million may be subject to a lockup agreement, which means you won't be able to touch it for 6 months. Not only that, but during those 6 months that $7.5 million is subject to market risk.' They'll say, 'Oh my God.' Different forms of equity get very different forms of tax treatments. This is the concept I try to hammer home."

WHO EARNS WHAT WHERE

But what are the norms? What is the median starting base salary for a senior Web designer in Duluth, for example, or an electronic data interchange specialist in Santa Fe?

A handy Web site called Salary.com (www.salary.com) will tell you. In the appropriate box on its home page, Salary.com lists every dot-com-related job title of possible interest to you, under seven headings:

- Internet and New Media
- IT — All
- IT — Computers, Hardware
- IT — Computers, Software
- IT — Computers, Executive Consulting
- IT — Computers, Manager
- IT — Computers, Networking

Enter the category closest to your career objective, then click on Location. You now have 322 metropolitan area options from which to choose. Let's see what the Internet and new-media salary situation is in Pensacola, Florida. Following is the range of job titles for which salary and job description information is available in that category and setting:

Art Director—Web	Designer II—Web
Associate Editor—Web	Designer III—Web
Associate Producer—Web	Director Human Resources
Associate Product Manager—Web	E-Commerce Customer Service Rep.
Business Development Associate	Editor—Web
Business Development Associate, Sr.	Editorial Assistant—Web
Business Development Manager	Electronic Data Interchange Specialist
Community Director—Web	Executive Producer—Web
Community Leader—Web	Graphical User Interface Programmer I
Community Specialist—Web	Graphical User Interface Programmer II
Content Engineer I—Web	Graphical User Interface Programmer III
Content Engineer II—Web	Inside Technical Sales
Content Engineer III—Web	Interface Design Director—Web
Content Specialist	Interface Designer—Web
Content Specialist, Sr.	Interface Designer, Sr.—Web
Copy Editor—Web	Intranet Applications Manager—Web
Creative Director—Web	Intranet Applications Specialist—Web
Data Warehouse Specialist	Intranet Applications Specialist, Sr.—Web
Designer I—Web	IT Contracts Manager

Line Producer I—Web
Line Producer II—Web
Line Producer III—Web
Manager Data Warehousing
Manager E-Commerce
Managing Editor—Web
Merchandising Manager—Web
Photo Editor—Web
Producer—Web
Product Management Director—Web
Product Manager—Web
Production Artist—Web
Production Assistant—Web
Section Editor—Web
Senior Business Development Manager
Senior Producer—Web
Senior Product Manager—Web
Software Quality Assurance

Software Quality Assurance, Sr.
Surfer—Web
Technical Producer I—Web
Technical Producer II—Web
Technical Producer III—Web
Top Content/Studios Executive—Web
Top Creative Executive—Web
Top Product Development Executive
Web Designer
Web Designer, Sr.
Web Security Administrator
Web Software Developer
Web Software Developer, Sr.
Webmaster
Writer I—Web
Writer II—Web
Writer III—Web

Pick a job title to investigate further. For fun, we'll select Surfer—Web. Choose it (or any other job title you want to know more about) and click Create Salary Report. On the day we checked, the report went as follows: "A typical Surfer–Web working in the Pensacola, Florida, metropolitan area is expected to earn a median base salary of $32,171. Half the people in this job are expected to earn between $32,730 and $35,291 (i.e., between the 25th and 75th percentiles). These numbers are based on national averages adjusted by geographic salary differentials." Below a graph plotting the salary figures is a Surfer–Web job description, along with minimum entry requirements: "Visits multiple Web sites to gather information. Requires a high school diploma with 0 to 2 years experience in the field or in a related area. Has knowledge of commonly used concepts, practices, and procedures within a particular field. Relies on instructions and preestablished guidelines to perform the functions of the job. Works under immediate supervision. Little creativity is required. Typically reports to a manager."

Use the Salary Wizard to estimate the median salary for your position and locale. Note: The existence of a job description and salary report is no assurance that suitable jobs exist in the metropolitan areas that interest you. Use the techniques described in Chapter 10.

LET THE HAGGLING BEGIN

Unless you are interviewing for your first permanent, full-time job, there should be some leeway in your level of compensation. Rule number one: Never initiate salary negotiations until you are relatively certain you have a job offer. But when you are asked about your salary history, answer concisely, including all bonuses and perquisites. If you think you were exploited or underpaid, don't even hint at it. Playing victim will almost invariably backfire on you.

If from the Salary Wizard or another source you know what salary range is being offered, you should aim a little above the midpoint. This will give you room to grow in the position before you are considered for a promotion down the road. To the question, "What kind of money are you expecting to make?" (or any variation thereof), you might answer "Well, my package at Bondex was $84,000. From the way you describe this job, I'd say it was worth about $94,000."

This seems reasonable. You're asking for a little more than a 10 percent boost, and you would seem to be worth it if you're the candidate getting the offer.

But let's say the job appears to be a stretch in the eyes of your prospective boss, but *you're* sure you can handle it. The response to that same question might be "I'm sure I can do the job, but I realize that (mention the perceived soft spot in your candidacy) might be new to me.

I'd be willing to start at $84,000—what I was making at Bondex. Then if in 3 months I were meeting your expectations, let's say my base would be raised to $94,000. And if I haven't met your expectations by that time, I'll leave."

This puts you at risk, but in a healthy kind of way. You are demonstrating the courage of your convictions in an all-or-nothing manner that is likely to elevate your candidacy to an offer. Don't make such a statement, however, unless you mean it and intend to follow through. Empty bravado will have you looking for another job within 3 months. The risk is not a huge one, though, because company policy, especially in larger companies, probably precludes such ad hoc agreements. Still, just making the proposal will cause your future boss to be less doubtful about your ability, and perhaps lead to a more generous offer.

Don't get boxed into a specific figure prematurely. Talk first in $5,000 to $10,000 ranges. If the interview has gone superbly, aim high and then negotiate. If you are in doubt about the range the employer is considering and are asked about your salary expectations, answer the question with one of your own. "Ah, I'm glad you brought up the subject of compensation. What range did you have in mind for the job?" Then negotiate from there.

But never make a decision at the interview—whether it's your first, second, or third. Say, "I appreciate your offer and will give it serious consideration. May I call you Tuesday (or 48 hours out) with my decision?" This gives you a chance to weigh this offer against any other you may be considering, as well as to reflect more thoroughly on this particular offer.

Searching for Skeletons

Before you leave, ask any questions about the organization and the position that are either hanging fire or to which you have not as yet received satisfactory answers. In a newer dot-com, for example, if there is a chance that the company's survival depends on the next round or two of funding, better to find out now rather than later.

Or, if the opening is not a new one, find out the circumstances under which your predecessor left. If you are told that the reason was one of "chemistry" or personality conflict, get to the bottom of it to be sure that the "personality" involved was not that of your new boss. Try to contact the person who held the job previously for firsthand information. If the two of you seem to share many of the same values and attitudes, you may want to reconsider the offer. If you have much in common with a previous employee whose attitude or philosophy was at odds with that of the company, you might well be guaranteeing yourself a brief tenure. Decide which is more important to you: those particular values or the job.

Their Money or Your Life

Before you jump at a generous offer, look carefully at the flip side. Don't give up in potential and prestige what you might be gaining in a monthly paycheck. Analyze the entire compensation package, including benefits and stock options, to be sure that a lower salary with excellent fringe benefits may not yield more for you in the long run. Ask your accountant to steer you through the stickier issues.

If you view this position as a plateau to greater professional rewards down the road, be sure the experience and accomplishments you stand to gain aren't of greater intrinsic value than a higher-paying position that may weaken your next résumé. And when all the evidence is in, count on your instincts and gut reaction to help deliver a decision in your best interests.

We wish you success in your e-career search. The Net is still a volatile world for job seekers—and probably will remain so for the next several years. Nevertheless, there are excellent companies out there, including some of the newer and smaller ones. Do your homework as comprehensively as you can, and there is little doubt that you will find a good professional home—and the best match for your talents, interests, energy level, and career goals.

APPENDIX

Stock Options and Restricted Stock

STOCK OPTIONS

Stock options are a very popular form of compensation to reward and retain key employees. While the financial benefits of stock options are very attractive, their tax treatment can be very complex. Because of all the tax rules governing stock options, early tax planning is that much more essential to maximize the benefits and avoid costly mistakes.

There are two types of employer stock options:

- Incentive stock options
- Nonqualified stock options

Incentive Stock Options (ISOs)

Incentive stock options (ISOs) usually allow you to purchase the stock of your employer at a future date without incurring a tax until you sell the stock. Typically, you are granted an ISO that permits you to purchase shares at a future date for a specified price (exercise price) that is expected

APPENDIX

ISO Example

Your employer granted you ISOs 4 years ago that allowed you to purchase 10,000 shares of the company stock at $10 per share. At the time of the grant, the stock was trading at $10 per share. You exercise the option 2 years later and purchase 10,000 shares when the stock is selling for $25 per share. You then sell the stock after waiting 12 months for $35 per share.

Your tax consequences are as follows:

- No regular tax cost at either the time of the grant or at the exercise of the option.
- AMT preference of $150,000 at the time of exercise (10,000 shares at $15 per share; the difference between the fair market value of $25 and the exercise price of $10).
- Long-term capital gain of $250,000 when the shares are sold (10,000 shares at $35 per share less your basis of $10 per share). Based on the maximum capital gain tax rate of 20 percent, your federal tax cost is $50,000.
- AMT negative preference of $150,000 at the time of the sale, which can reduce or eliminate the AMT liability, if any, in the year of the sale.

Warning: As this example indicates, your AMT preference will be $150,000 at the time you exercise the options. This could result in an AMT liability as high as $42,000 ($150,000 at the AMT rate of 28 percent).

to be lower than the actual market price on that date. The following are the key tax consequences from the granting and exercising of ISOs:

- There is no regular income tax cost when the ISO is granted or exercised.
- An alternative minimum tax (AMT) liability can result due to the preference item on the difference between the fair market

value of the stock and the exercise price on the date of the exercise.
- Exercise and sale of the stock within 2 years after the option is granted is a disqualifying disposition that results in the gain being taxed as ordinary income.
- You will qualify for long-term capital gain treatment if you hold the exercised shares for more than 12 months and more than 2 years have elapsed since the issuance of the grant. If you fail to meet either holding requirement, you will have ordinary income when sold.

You should be aware of the following additional rules when you exercise ISOs:

- You must remain an employee of the corporation from the time the option is granted until 3 months before the option is exercised.
- The fair market value of the shares exercisable in any 1 year cannot exceed $100,000 based on the grant date value. Any amount in excess would be a nonqualified stock option.
- A portion of your ISOs can become nonqualified stock options if, as a result of an initial public offering, you are able to accelerate future options whose total original fair market value exceeds $100,000.

SHOULD YOU EXERCISE EARLY? There can be both significant tax advantages of exercising your grant before the expiration date as well as potential tax costs of the early exercise. Use careful planning to find the right balance.

The advantages of exercising your grant early include the ability to:

- *Start your holding period now* so that you can sell the shares after 12 months and receive long-term capital gain treatment on the sale.

APPENDIX

> **Opportunity to Reduce AMT Preference**
>
> Consider exercising your grant during periods when the stock price dips so long as you are confident that the long-term outlook remains strong. This way your tax preference amount remains small and you can avoid an AMT liability.

- *Reduce your AMT* preference by exercising the grant when the spread between the fair market value per share and the exercise price is small.
- *Minimize your AMT* liability by annually exercising just enough shares so that the preference item is not large enough to trigger the AMT.

The disadvantages of exercising your grant early are primarily that it will:

- *Accelerate the funds* you will need to exercise the grant.
- *Expose you to a loss* if the value of the shares drops below the price you paid to exercise the shares.
- *Create a tax cost* if the preference item from the exercise generates an AMT liability.

In order to decide when to exercise your grant and how many shares you should purchase, you must first do the following:

- *Project both your regular tax and AMT* for the year so you can determine the number of shares you can exercise without incurring a current-year AMT liability.
- *Determine the amount of cash you will need* to exercise the shares and, if necessary, consider a cashless exercise using existing shares you own to maximize the total number of shares you will eventually own.

> ## Nonqualified Stock Option Example
>
> Using the same figures from the preceding ISO example, upon exercise of a nonqualified option you would be required to report ordinary income of $150,000 (10,000 shares at $25 per share fair market value less the $10 per share exercise cost). Your basis in the stock would now be $25 per share since you have recognized the income. One year later when you sell the stock for $35 per share, you will recognize a capital gain of $100,000 (10,000 shares at $35 less your basis of $25 per share). The total maximum federal tax cost related to the exercise of the options and subsequent sale of the stock is computed as follows:
>
> | | |
> |---|---:|
> | Tax upon exercise of options at 39.6% | $59,400 |
> | Tax when you sell the shares at 20% | 20,000 |
> | Total federal tax cost | $79,400 |
>
> **Note:** This example does not include social security or medicare tax that would be assessed on your ordinary income.

- *Project multiple scenarios* assuming various future stock prices. This will better allow you to determine whether you should exercise a large block of shares now and pay the current-year AMT tax with the potential for greater future tax savings.

Nonqualified Stock Options

Unlike an ISO, the exercise of a nonqualified stock option will result in taxable ordinary income to the extent that the fair market value of the stock at the time you exercise the grant exceeds the exercise price. When a nonqualified option is granted, you do not have taxable income unless the value of the option is readily ascertainable, which is usually not the case.

APPENDIX

Restricted Stock Election Section 83(b)

If you receive restricted stock as compensation, you have an opportunity to make an election to recognize ordinary income now so that you can receive the following potential tax benefits:

- *Convert future stock appreciation* from ordinary income into capital gain income, thereby gaining the advantage of the lower capital gain tax rate.
- *Avoid greater ordinary income* that potentially would be recognized when the restrictions lift.

This election, under Internal Revenue Code Section 83(b), is especially beneficial if:

- The income you must report will be small based on the fair market value of the restricted stock, and
- The potential appreciation of the stock is great.

The disadvantages of this election include:

- Prepayment of tax in the current year.
- No tax benefits *will be gained* if the stock doesn't appreciate.
- Tax you pay due to the election can't be refunded if you forfeit the stock or if the value of the stock decreases after the election is made. However, you will have a capital loss at the time of the sale of the stock, since your basis will be higher.

Section 83(b) Timing Alert

The Section 83(b) election must be made within 30 days after the stock is transferred to you.

Benefits of Making Section 83(b) Election

Using the assumptions in the text, the following summary compares the difference between making the election or not.

If you make the Section 83(b) election:

- You have $45,000 of additional compensation this year based on the fair market value of $1.50 per share times the 30,000 shares you were given.
- Your basis in the stock is $1.50 per share, the compensation you reported.
- Your holding period for determining eligibility for long-term capital gain treatment begins on the day you receive the stock.
- You will realize a long-term capital gain of $495,000 (30,000 shares at $18 per share less your basis of $1.50 per share) when you sell the stock.

If you don't make the election:

- You do not have any compensation this year when you receive the shares.
- You will have compensation of $300,000 2 years later when the company goes public and the restriction is lifted, based on the fair market value of $10 per share for 30,000 shares.
- Your basis becomes $10 per share when you realize the additional compensation and your holding period starts on that day.
- You will have a long-term capital gain of $240,000 when you sell the stock (30,000 shares at $18 per share less your basis of $10 per share).

continued on next page

	Tax Comparison:	
	If you make the election	If you don't make the election
Tax on:		
Compensation	$18,000	$120,000
Capital gains	99,000	48,000
Medicare tax	653	4,350
Total tax	$117,653	$172,350
Tax savings	$54,697	

SECTION 83(B) EXAMPLE   As an example, assume you are offered 30,000 shares of company stock with a fair market value of $1.50 per share at no cost to you if you join the management team of an early-stage nonpublic company. The shares are subject to a substantial risk of forfeiture since you must give back the shares if you leave the company during the next 3 years, unless an initial public offering (IPO) occurs earlier. It is expected that the company will have an IPO within 2 years, at which time all restrictions lapse. There is great enthusiasm for the company, and it is projected that the shares will have a fair market value of $10 per share at the IPO. You will sell the stock more than 1 year after the IPO for $18 per share.

The box above shows the benefit of making the Section 83(b) election. In this example, your federal tax savings would be $54,697, assuming a rounded maximum tax rate of 40 percent for your compensation and 20 percent for the long-term capital gain element.

Glossary

analog   electronic device that uses a system of unlimited variables to measure or represent the flow of data. Radios are analog because variable sound waves are used to carry data from transmitter to receiver.

applet   small software application or utility built to perform one task. Often used as components within a larger system.

artificial intelligence (AI)   branch of computer science concerned with equipping computer systems with humanlike thought, logic, and learning capabilities.

backbone   largest of communication lines on the Internet that connect cities and major telecommunication centers. Made of fiber-optic cable bundles that have the capacity to handle massive amounts of information.

bandwidth   amount of data that can be transmitted through an Internet connection, usually measured in bits per second (bps).

Bluetooth   short-range wireless networking technology that uses radio waves to share information. Bluetooth can transmit both voice and data over a short range, is very small, and uses very little power. The technology is ideal for small electronic devices such as digital cameras.

broadband high-speed Internet connection, such as through a cable modem or digital subscriber line (DSL), that is "always on," which means the data connection is not broken until the computer is turned off.

data packet multiple pieces of data that have been joined together and treated as a single entity when passed between network sites.

DHTML dynamic HTML, a Web technology that permits changes to be made to a Web page that were once considered unchangeable once the page has loaded—such as text, page style, font, color, and position. Allows images to appear and disappear, and content to move around freely inside the screen.

dialup modem Internet connection.

digital electronic device that uses a limited, predetermined numbering system to measure or represent the flow of data. Modern computers are digital because they use combinations of fixed binary digits (0s and 1s) to represent all data.

digital subscriber line (DSL) technology used to transmit digital data on regular copper telephone wires to provide connections to the Internet or local area networks. Allows analog voice phone calls and digital signals to coexist on the same telephone wires.

domain name identifier for an Internet or Web server, or group of servers, from a single company or institution.

downlink data sent from a satellite to an earth station.

downstream data sent from the Internet to a user.

encryption encoding a file to make it unreadable except by those with the appropriate key to decode it.

GLOSSARY

Ethernet local area network protocol created by Xerox in the 1970s.

extensible markup language (*see* XML.)

extranet computer network (usually an extension of a company intranet) that shares information and facilitates communication between an organization and its partners or clients.

fiber optics use of light to transmit data, video, and voice. Fiber-optic cable has a much higher bandwidth and carries signals over much longer distances than cable. It is also lighter, easier to install, and provides better security.

file transfer protocol (FTP) data transfer tool that facilitates sending files from one computer to another, downloading software, and saving Web pages, regardless of computer make or operating system.

firewall security mechanism that guards a computer or a network of computers from intrusion by unauthorized parties via Internet connections.

gigabit one billion bits.

gigaPoP network access point that allows a connection, or PoP (point of presence), to Internet backbones at speeds of 1 billion bits per second or higher.

hertz measurement of the number of times per second a radio wave changes direction or completes a cycle. One kilohertz (KHz) equals 1000 cycles per second; one megahertz (MHz) equals 1 million cycles per second; and a gigahertz (GHz) is 1 billion cycles per second.

home page first or main page visitors see upon directing their browsers to a Web site or company intranet.

host server main contact computer to which other computers connect to access information from that network.

hyperlink words, pictures, or icon (often highlighted) embedded within a Web or intranet page's HTML code that contain connections to related

GLOSSARY

Web pages or elements. Users can simply click a hyperlink and their Web browser automatically accesses the related page or document.

hypertext markup language (HTML) code used to create Web and intranet pages. HTML lets a browser know how to display and format a given Web page's fonts, hyperlinks, and other elements.

hypertext transfer protocol (HTTP) set of rules that governs the exchange of graphics, text, and multimedia files over the Internet.

Internet worldwide network of computers linked by vast networks of fiber-optic cable and public communications networks (especially telephone networks) that includes the World Wide Web.

Internet Protocol (IP) set of rules that govern the transmission of data from one computer to another over the Internet.

Internet Protocol (IP) address numeric address used to locate computers on a Transmission Control Protocol/Internet Protocol (TCP/IP) network. Address includes four groups of numbers of up to three digits each, with each set separated by periods.

Internet service provider (ISP) company that arranges for users to dial into its computers, which in turn are connected to the Internet, usually for a monthly fee.

intranet computer network established by companies and organizations to facilitate internal communication and information sharing.

local area network (LAN) group of computers, usually in one building or office, physically connected in a manner that lets them communicate and interact with one another.

microbrowsers software used by wireless devices to access and display Web sites. Cell phones and other devices use microbrowsers to display Web information on their small screens.

modem acronym for "modulator/demodulator." Modems translate digital information from a computer into analog information trans-

GLOSSARY

mitted through a telephone line. Modems also translate analog data coming from a telephone line back into digital information.

Multipurpose Internet Mail Extensions (MIME)   protocol that enhances e-mail, allowing it to contain color graphics and a variety of fonts and typefaces.

network interface card (NIC)   circuit board that lets your computer connect to a network. Sometimes called a *network adapter*.

packet   chunk of data transmitted from one computer to another on a network or across the Internet, and containing three parts: (1) the actual data being routed; (2) an address for routing the data; and (3) information that helps correct errors that may occur as the data is transmitted.

packet switching   to break down data being transmitted over a network or the Internet into smaller parts to permit faster transmission. When the packets arrive at their destination, they reassemble into the original data form.

plug-in   software applications and scripts that add functionality to another application. Plug-ins added to Netscape Navigator, for example, enable it to display content in an unfamiliar format.

post office protocol (POP)   set of rules that allow mail servers to send and retrieve e-mail and communicate with compatible e-mail programs.

protocol   standardized "language" that lets hardware devices and software applications communicate with one another.

robot (bot)   software programs that automatically perform specified computer tasks.

router   hardware device that helps join computers on the Internet and moves data packets from one local area network to another.

scalability   process of adapting a system to accommodate the demands placed on it. (To "scale up" means to add hardware; to "scale out" means to add software.)

GLOSSARY

search engine   software that searches electronic documents for specific keywords or phrases, indexes what it finds, and returns a list of locations where the documents can be found.

server   computer that holds data used by a number of different computers on a network.

Simple Mail Transfer Protocol (SMTP)   basic mechanism for moving e-mail, consisting of two parts: (1) a "header," which carries the date and time of the message, the route it took to reach its destination, and the addresses of the sender and receiver; and (2) the "body," which carries the actual message.

spam   unsolicited and usually unwelcome e-mail messages containing anything from advertisements to illicit material.

spider   robot instructed by user input to automatically find Web pages and catalog them in the database of a search engine.

streaming media   audio and video data transmitted from a server to an end user and displayed on-screen as it arrives.

switch   device used to forward data packets from one segment of a network to another.

tag   an HTML command. Tags are enclosed in "more-than" and "less-than" signs called *directives*. An end tag must accompany most tags to indicate to the browser the end of a specific HTML command.

T1 line   high-speed data connection, often used to link large computer networks, which can transmit a digital signal at 1.544 megabits per second (Mbps).

transceiver   piece of equipment, such as a modem or an antenna, that acts as both a transmitter and a receiver.

Transmission Control Protocol/Internet Protocol (TCP/IP)   group of protocols used to govern communication between Internet-connected computers. TCP divides data that is traveling on the Internet into small

GLOSSARY

packets. IP assigns each packet an address. As packets travel from router to router, TCP checks a packet for errors, and the router uses the IP to forward the packet to its destination. TCP then reassembles the packets into their proper sequence when they reach their destination.

transponder circuitry on a satellite that receives the uplink signal, amplifies it, and retransmits it as the downlink signal.

T3 line high-speed data connection, often used to link large computer networks, which can transmit a digital signal at 44.746 megabits per second (Mbps).

uniform resource locator (URL) networkwide address used by a Web browser for locating a specific document. The URL includes a Web server's domain name and the specific file name for the Web page being accessed.

uplink data sent from an earth station to a satellite.

upstream data sent from a user to the Internet.

Usenet giant bulletin board on the Internet, consisting of user news, e-mail, and forums that discuss thousands of topics. Usenet newsgroups can be accessed through the Internet.

virus computer program designed to replicate itself and spread itself among computers, causing a variety of harmful effects such as loss of data.

Web browser software program that lets computers communicate over the World Wide Web and intranets.

Web server software running on a PC, Linux-based machine, or Unix computer that understands HTML code. Can also refer to the computer running Web server software.

wide area network (WAN) group of computers connected by satellite or leased line across a wide area, usually including several local area networks (LANs), of which the Internet is the ultimate example.

GLOSSARY

Wireless Application Protocol (WAP)   standard developers use WAP to create Internet content that can be accessed by cell phones and other wireless devices.

World Wide Web   graphical interface for the Internet that lets users access text, graphics, sound, and multimedia data.

worm   destructive program used to spread computer viruses, and containing code that replicates itself until it fills the drive of a network, causing it to malfunction.

XML (Extensible Markup Language)   a mechanism for describing the structure and organization of texts within any domain. Permits content to be presented in multiple formats for different consumers.

Bibliography

The books and magazines annotated below provide additional specialized information for various aspects of Internet and job-search topics covered in the 12 chapters of *The Dot-Com Decision*.

USEFUL BOOKS

Bartlett, Joseph W., *Fundamentals of Venture Capital*. Madison Books, Lanham, MD, 1999. One of the top lawyers in the venture capital field covers fundamental issues facing the would-be entrepreneur. Well-written, straightforward guide.

Clark, Peter J., and Stephen Neill, *Net Value: Valuing Dot-Com companies—Uncovering the Reality Behind the Hype*. American Management Association, New York, 2001. Insightful, pragmatic look at the dot-com phenomenon, including the crash of 2000 and what kinds of companies are best positioned to survive the ensuing shakeout.

Crowther, Karmen, *Researching Your Way to a Good Job*. John Wiley & Sons, New York, 1993. Provides tools and techniques to examine potential employers and jobs, and job-related information on other communities, if you intend to relocate.

BIBLIOGRAPHY

Dikel, Margaret Rilley, and Frances Roehm, *The Guide to Internet Job Searching*. VGM Career Horizons, Chicago, 2000. How to target the most interesting jobs in the most promising companies, and how to apply for those jobs with confidence—online or on paper.

Earle, Nick, and Peter Keen, *From Dot.com to .Profit*. Jossey-Bass, San Francisco, 2000. How to build the brands, perfect the logistics, provide the services, and anticipate online trends—all the practical advice managers need to create business plans that work in the new economy.

Henderson, Harry, *Career Opportunities in Computers and Cyberspace*. Facts on File, New York, 1999. Examines 70 jobs in the computer field.

Holden, Greg, *Starting an Online Business for Dummies*. IDG Books Worldwide, Inc., Foster City, CA, 2000. User-friendly guide with step-by-step advice for developing a business model; building a secure, effective e-business; marketing your site aggressively; and finding business tips and services online. Includes CD-ROM with software for shareware graphics program, Web-page creation program, accounting program, and more.

Joel, Lewin G., *Every Employee's Guide to the Law*. Pantheon Books, New York, 1993. From coping with on-the-job problems to negotiating severance pay, this easy-to-read, concise, and reassuring guide explains everything you need to know about your rights as an employee—and what action you can take if your employer is violating them.

Kador, John, *Internet Jobs: The Complete Guide to Finding the Hottest Jobs on the Net*. McGraw-Hill, Boston, 1999. Insider's guide, written by a computer-industry veteran. Top 100 Internet employers; 50 top cities; guidance on certifications.

Kobler, Ronald D. (ed.) et al., *How the Internet Works*. Sandhills Publishing Company, Lincoln, NE, 2001. Subtitled "The Illustrated Book of the Internet" because abstract principles are defined graphically as well as verbally. Complete explanations of such inside concepts as access devices, delivery options, Internet service, providers, protocols, applications, and robotics.

Liberty, Jesse, *Complete Idiot's Guide to a Career in Computer Programming*. Que, Carmel, IN, 1999. Everything you need to know to get started. Covers the work environment, alternative career paths, and skills needed to be a professional computer programmer.

Pottruck, David S., and Terry Pearce, *Clicks and Mortar*. Jossey-Bass, San Francisco, 2000. What it takes to build a high-growth organization in today's electronic environment. Through dozens of examples from both start-ups and *Fortune* 500 companies, the authors show how organizations can marry technology with the best qualities of people to create the perfect environment to foster success.

Strunk, William, Jr., and E.B. White, *Elements of Style,* 3rd ed. Macmillan Publishing Co., Inc., New York, 1979. The best small book in print on making words count. Useful for résumé writing assistance.

Tarrant, John, with Paul Fargis, *Perks and Parachutes,* 2nd ed. Stonesong Press (Random House), New York, 1997. The best book available on contract negotiation—what should and should not be part of any employment deal. Includes compensation terms, benefit packages, how job performance is judged, when you can be fired, and your rights after you leave the company.

Vaughn, Joan, *Webmaster Career Starter*. Learning Express, New York, 1999. Training programs, financial aid, how to land your first job, and how to succeed once you've landed the job. Excellent introduction to a Webmaster's career.

Wilson, Robert F., *Better Résumés for Executives and Professionals,* 4th ed., Barron's Educational Series, Inc., Hauppauge, NY, 2000. Tips on utilizing dozens of online job-search links; detailed advice for locating targeted jobs; more than 100 model résumés and cover letters that focus on business management and professional positions.

Wilson, Robert F., *Conducting Better Job Interviews,* 2nd ed., Barron's Educational Series, Inc., Hauppauge, NY, 1997. Secrets from the employer's side of the desk. What new managers are taught about how to choose the best person for the job.

Wilson, Robert F. and Erik Rambusch, *Conquer Interview Objections*. John Wiley & Sons, New York, 1994. Writes Francis "Buck" Rodgers, author of *The IBM Way*: "Accomplishes the most important objective a job seeker has in today's competitive marketplace: to clearly portray one's value-added capabilities. . . . A practical and exciting roadmap."

Wilson, Robert F., *Interview to Win Your First Job* (video and workbook program), 3rd ed., Wilson McLeran, Inc., Saxtons River, VT, 2000. Video and workbook program for college students preparing for their first full-time, permanent job search. ("Very professional. . . . This is probably the best tape on the subject this reviewer has seen."—*The Library Journal*)

Zinsser, William. *On Writing Well*. HarperCollins Publishers, New York, 1990. Sound advice for anyone utilizing the written word. Dozens of examples of good writing, buttressed by sound analysis.

BIBLIOGRAPHY

USEFUL MAGAZINES

Business 2.0. Published biweekly by Imagine Media, Inc., 150 North Hill Drive, Brisbane, CA. Also available online: www.business2.com

Industry Standard. "The newsmagazine of the Internet industry." Published by Standard Media International, 415 Pacific Avenue, San Francisco, CA. Also available online: www.thestandard.com

Red Herring. "The business of innovation." Published by Red Herring Communications, 1950 Bryant Street, San Francisco, CA. Also available online: www.redherring.com

Index

Abboud, Joseph, 94
About.com, 115
Acquisitions, 29–30 (*See also* Partnerships)
Administrative Resources Network, 124
Advanced Research Projects Agency (ARPA), 13
AllThingsPhoto.com, 53–54
Alpert, Gary, 10–12, 87–88, 185
Amazon.com, 33, 37, 41, 54, 55
America Online, 18, 26, 28
The American Institute of Graphic Arts, 112
American Standard Code for Information Interchange (ASCII), 145, 146
Andreessen, Marc, 18, 19, 20–21
Angel investors, 65–66, 70
Animation Magazine, 113
Animators, computer, 112–113
Applications programmers, 104
Applied Communications Research, 4

ARPA (Advanced Research Projects Agency), 13
ARPANET, 15–16, 17
"As We May Think" (Bush), 12
ASCII (American Standard Code for Information Interchange), 145, 146
Association for Computing Machinery, 100, 107
A.T. Kearney, 26
@Home Network, 24
AT&T, 15, 24
Aweida Venture Management, 65, 67–68

Benefits, employee, 92–94, 189, 191
Benson, Teddy, 63
Berners-Lee, Tim, 16, 17
Bizjournals.com, 170
Bolt, Beranek and Newman, 15
Bonuses as compensation, 189, 191
Brackenbury, Sheila, 148

INDEX

Broadcom, 28
Brod, Ernie, 96
Bush, Vannevar, 12
Business2.0, 6
Business incubators, 62–65, 69, 70
Business models, 5, 8–9, 52–54, 83
Business strategy, 36–37, 50, 51, 55, 57–58
Buy.com, 34–35
Byrne, Patrick, 55

Capitalists, venture, 60–62, 65, 67–71
Career opportunities, 97–117, 119–140
CareerBuilder, 189
Carpenter, Candice, 74
CDI@Work, 92
Central Florida Innovation Corporation (CFIC), 62–65
CFIC (Central Florida Innovation Corporation), 62–65
Challenger, Gray & Christmas, 38
Chandler, Alfred D., Jr., 13–14
Cisco, 6
Clark, Peter J., 6
Co-location companies, 25
Colony, George, 92
CommissionJunction.com, 40–41
Community for Software Engineers, 108
Companies, research of, 94–96, 169–170, 182, 186, 196–197
CompaniesOnline, 170
Compensation negotiation, 189–197 (*See also* Earnings; Stock)
Computer animators, 112–113
Computer engineers, 98–100
Computer support careers, 116–117
Contracts for employment, 190–192
Corporate culture, 91–96, 121, 135, 138, 169–170, 182

Corporate Technology Communications, 5, 28, 36, 59, 94–95, 178, 190
Cortada, James W., 13–14
Cousin, Amandilo, 27
Crincoli, Nick, 192
Cummings, Gordon, 159–161

DaimlerChrysler, 26
Deshpande, Desh, 73
Desktop publishing, 113–115
DesktopPublishingEzines, 115
Development engineers, 99
Digital Media Online, 113
Donovan, K.C., 24–26, 181
Dress, office, 94, 182
Driscoll, Steve, 13
Drugstore.com, 36
Dubois, Arnold, 134–137

e-commerce, 33–46
Earnings:
    hardware systems, 100, 102, 103, 127
    Internet jobs, 124, 130, 189–197
    new media, 111, 113, 115, 134, 137
    software systems, 106, 108, 120
eBay, 33, 37–38, 50, 51
eCompany, 7, 37
Education requirements:
    hardware, 99–100, 101, 102–103, 127
    Internet, 86–88, 123, 130, 192, 195
    media, 111, 113, 115, 134, 135, 137
    software, 105–106, 108, 120, 121
Elliot, Paul, 42–44
eMarketer.com, 33
Employment:
    careers with dot-com, 97–117
    contracts for, 190–192
    good employers, criteria for, 94–96

220

INDEX

Employment (*cont.*)
   hiring, 73–80
   Internet business success, 10–12
   marketing for specific, 169–174
   personality attributes of computer employees, 88–89, 121, 125, 131, 135, 138
   résumés for target, 144–145
   temporary workers, 124
   working for dot-coms, 83–96
   YouKnowBest expectations of, 78
   (*See also* Job searches)
End user support jobs, 116–117
Enterasys Networks, 28, 29–31
Ernst & Young, 31
eToys, 34
Excite.com, 23–24
Excite@Home, 24, 28, 41, 172

First Internet Bank of Indiana, 20
Fischer, Jeff, 45
Flynn, Brian, 66–67
Ford, 45–46
Formats of résumés, 145–148
Forrester Research, 45, 92
FoundStone, 31
Fox, Richard, 64
The Free Online Dictionary of Computing, 57n
Fulmer, Alan, 49–58, 60, 63–69, 73–79
Funding procurement, 59–71

Gates, Bill, 13, 49, 50
GeekCorps, 90
General Motors, 45–46
Gladwell, Malcolm, 91
Globix Corporation, 24–25, 28, 181
Google.com, 3, 87, 92–93, 172
Gopher system, 17, 29
Graphic designers, 110–112
Greenwald, Gerald, 26

Gula, Ron, 29–31

Haas Marketing Group, 5
Hailstorm, 50
Half.com, 55
Hanash, Alain, 8–9
Hanash, Patrick, 8–9
Hardware systems careers, 98–103
Health Central, 36
Heinlein, Robert, 57n
Hogan, Gordon, 64
Home Depot, 34, 35
HomeFair, 173
Hoover's Online, 169
HotJobs, 36, 148
Hotwired.com, 18
Hydra crawler, 54

Incubators, business, 62–65, 69, 70
Information interviewing, 173–174
Insala Group, 9
Institute for Certification of Computing Professionals, 102, 107
Institute of Electronic and Electrical Engineers, 102
Interface designers, 109–110
International Data Corporation, 44–45
International Programmers Guild, 107
Internet2, 3–4
Internet business, 3–12, 23–32, 33–46
   (*See also* Companies, research of)
Internet development, 3–4, 12–21, 49
Internships, 87–88, 144
Interviews, 75–79, 173–174, 175–188
Investment procurement, 59–71
Irish, Kelly, 149–152, 154–155
iVillage, 74, 190

James, William, 182

INDEX

Job descriptions, 97–117, 119–140, 192–195
Job searches:
  accepting a position, 186, 197
  interviews, 75–79, 173–174, 175–188
  interviews with employers, 178
  networking, 173–174, 185
  recruiting firms, 170–172
  résumés, 143–174 (*See also* Employment)
JobBank, 148
John, Richard R., 13
Johnson, Richard, 36
Joint ventures, 35 (*See also* Partnerships)
JollyRoger.com, 28, 39–41
Juniper, 6
Jupiter Research, 41–42

Katz, Jon, 92
Keenan, Vernon, 8–9
King, Stephen, 20, 41
Kleinrock, Leonard, 15
Korsakoff, Alex P., 164–166
Kroll Associates, 96

Labor Statistics, U.S. Bureau of, 38
Languages, computer, 99, 104, 105
Larson, Paul, 45
LawVantage.com, 27
Linux, Red Hat, 40
Listen.com, 28
Loiacono, Christopher, 191–192
LookSmart, 28, 172
Loudcloud, Inc., 20–21
Lowell, William, 167–168
Lycos, 28, 172

Management Recruiters International, 94, 171
Marketing positions, 97, 116

Markets and dot-coms, 5, 54–57
McCoy, Terence, 37
McGucken, Elliot, 39–41
Me By Me (Pets.com Sock Puppet), 37
Media, 3, 14, 17, 27–28
Media, new, jobs, 110–115, 134–140
Mergers, 26–27 (*See also* Partnerships)
Meyer, Lisa, 5
Michael Lerner Productions, 25
Microsoft, 7, 18, 49, 50, 51
MIT Sloan School of Management, 92
Models, business, 5, 8–9, 52–54, 83
Mohit, Farhad, 35
Monster.com, 148, 151
More.com, 36
Mosaic Web browser, 18
The Motley Fool.com, 45
Motorola, 35
Multicity.com, 8–9

Napster, 20, 36, 43
A Nation Transformed by Information (Chandler and Cortada, eds.), 13–14, 13n
National Science Foundation, 17
.NET strategy, 50, 51
Netscape, 18, 25
NetValue: Valuing Dot-Com Companies (Clark), 6
Network Security Wizards, 29–30
Networking, 11, 132–133, 173–174, 185
New South Ventures, 69
Niche markets, 54–57
Nonqualified stock options, 203

Office environments, 91–95, 121, 138, 182 (*See also* Corporate culture)
OpenMind Publishing Group, 42–44
Options, stock, 190, 191, 192, 199–203
Oracle, 28
Overstock.com, 55

INDEX

Packet-switching networks, 14–15
Partnerships, 24–27, 29–30, 34–37, 40–41, 50, 51, 130–134
Perks and Parachutes (Tarrant), 191
Personality attributes, computer jobs, 88–89, 121, 125, 131, 135, 138
Pets.com, 37
Production engineers, 99
Professional organizations:
    hardware systems, 100, 102, 103
    new media, 112, 113, 115
    software systems, 106–107, 108
Programmers, 103–107, 120–123
Publishing, 20, 41–44, 113–115
Pure plays, 28, 34

Quality Assurance Institute, 100
Quality assurance jobs, 99, 123–126

Rand, Paul, 5, 36–37, 59, 94–95, 178, 190–191
Recruitment firms, 170–172
Red Hat Linux, 40
Restricted stock election section 83(b), 204–206
Résumés, 143–174, 176–177
ReturnBuy.com, 55
Richard A. Eisner and Co., 191
Riding the Bullet (King), 20, 41
Ridley, Antoinette, 162–163
Rising Star Internships, 87
Ritter, Otto, 51, 63
Roark, Phillip, 9
Romita, Tessa, 6
Russell Reynolds Associates, 88–89

Sagdahl, Paul, 156–158
Salary (*See* Earnings; Stock)
Salary.com, 192–195
Sans Institute, 31

Santiago, Anibal, 63
Schlossberger, Edwin, 66–67
Scholastic, online publishing, 42
Schonfeld, Erick, 7
Schultz, Brad, 42
Schurman, Kyle, 35
Sealey, Peter, 5
"Second Coming" (Schonfeld), 7
Security, 29–31, 35, 96
Shuchman, Lisa, 42
Smart Computing, 35
SmartBargains.com, 55
Society for Technical Communication, Inc., 103, 129
Software systems careers, 31, 103–110
Spiderweb effect, 31–32
Sputnik, 13–14
Stanford Research Institute, 15
Starr, Martin, 44
Staubly, John, 63
Stein, Becky, 89
Stock:
    employees holding, 77, 93, 189
    funding strategy, 60–61
    options, 190, 191, 192, 199–203
    restricted stock election section 83(b), 204–206
Stranger in a Strange Land (Heinlein), 57n
Strategy, business, 36–37, 50, 51, 55, 57–58
Strategy, funding, 60–63
Systems analysts, 100–102, 107
Systems programmers, 104–105

Tarrant, John, 191
Taxes on stocks, 190–192, 199–206
Taylor, T. Shawn, 94
Technical writers, 102–103, 127–130
Technology:
    Hydra crawler, 54
    improvement of interaction, 7, 24, 52

INDEX

Technology (*cont.*)
   Internet2, 3–4
   .NET strategy, 50, 51
   pre-wired communities, 67–68
   strategy based on, 36–37, 55
Telephone interviews, 176
Temp 24/7, 124
Temp NYC, 124
Temporary workers, 92, 124
TheoryNet, 16
Thomas, Owen, 37
Thomson Corporation, 42
3DSite, 113
Ticketmaster, 38
Time Warner, 26, 41–42
Tomlinson, Ray, 16
Toney, Fred, 36
Toys-R-Us, 34
Trantolo, Vince, 66–67

University of California, 15
University of Illinois, 18
University of Minnesota, 17
University of Utah, 15
University of Wisconsin, 16
Unix, 16
U.S. Bureau of Labor Statistics, 38, 97
Usenet, 16

Venture capitalists, 60–62, 65, 67–71

Verizon, 24
Vicunez, Ron, 120–123
Volunteer work, 90, 144

Wakin, Daniel J., 124
Wal-Mart, 34, 35, 54
Ward, Jay, 130–134
Web DNA, 88–89
Weinstein, Bob, 90
WetFeet.com, 10–12, 87–88, 173, 185
The WetFeet.com Insider Guide, Version 2000, 27–28
Whistler, Mark, 127–130
Whitaker, Barbara, 55
Whitman, Meg, 51
Wight, Risa, 63
Wight, Rob, 49–52, 60–63, 75–76
Wireless programmers, 105, 106
Workplaces, 91–95, 121, 138, 182 (*See also* Corporate culture)
The WorkSite.Com, 106

Yahoo, 28, 172–173
YouKnowBest, 51–58, 60–71, 73–80
Young, Eric, 51
Young, Tyrone, 123–126

Zuckerman, Ethan, 90

About the Author

Robert F. Wilson has specialized in career management for more than 20 years as a workshop leader, executive search consultant, outplacement counselor, and contributor to Internet resource providers. He is president of Wilson McLeran, Inc., in Saxtons River, Vermont. Wilson is the author of the award-winning career transition program *Job-Bridge®* and the writer and producer of the videotape *Interview to Win Your First Job*. His previous books include *Your Career in Healthcare, Better Résumés for Executives and Professionals, Conducting Better Job Interviews,* and *Success Without College: Careers in Sports, Fitness, and Recreation.*